W9-BEU-893

GLOBALVIEWPOINTS

Privacy

DATE

JUANITA HIGH SCHOOL
10601 N.E. 132ND ST.
KIRKLAND, WA 98034

Other Books of Related Interest:

At Issue Series

Current Controversies Series

Opposing Viewpoints Series

Privacy

Noël Merino, Book Editor

GREENHAVEN PRESS
A part of Gale, Cengage Learning

Farmington Hills, Mich • San Francisco • New York • Waterville, Maine
Meriden, Conn • Mason, Ohio • Chicago

GALE
CENGAGE Learning

Elizabeth Des Chenes, *Director, Content Strategy*
Cynthia Sanner, *Publisher*
Douglas Dentino, *Manager, New Product*

© 2014 Greenhaven Press, a part of Gale, Cengage Learning

WCN: 01-100-101

Gale and Greenhaven Press are registered trademarks used herein under license.

For more information, contact:
Greenhaven Press
27500 Drake Rd.
Farmington Hills, MI 48331-3535
Or you can visit our Internet site at gale.cengage.com

ALL RIGHTS RESERVED.
No part of this work covered by the copyright herein may be reproduced, transmitted, stored, or used in any form or by any means graphic, electronic, or mechanical, including but not limited to photocopying, recording, scanning, digitizing, taping, Web distribution, information networks, or information storage and retrieval systems, except as permitted under Section 107 or 108 of the 1976 United States Copyright Act, without the prior written permission of the publisher.

For product information and technology assistance, contact us at

Gale Customer Support, 1-800-877-4253
For permission to use material from this text or product, submit all requests online at www.cengage.com/permissions

Further permissions questions can be emailed to permissionrequest@cengage.com

Articles in Greenhaven Press anthologies are often edited for length to meet page require-ments. In addition, original titles of these works are changed to clearly present the main thesis and to explicitly indicate the author's opinion. Every effort is made to ensure that Greenhaven Press accurately reflects the original intent of the authors. Every effort has been made to trace the owners of copyrighted material.

Cover image copyright © Petar Paunchev/Shutterstock.com.

LIBRARY OF CONGRESS CATALOGING-IN-PUBLICATION DATA

Privacy / Noël Merino, book editor.
    pages cm. -- (Global viewpoints)
    Includes bibliographical references and index.
    ISBN 978-0-7377-6912-8 (hardcover) -- ISBN 978-0-7377-6913-5 (pbk.)
    1. Privacy. 2. Secrecy. 3. Surveillance detection. I. Merino, Noël.
    BF637.P74P738 2014
    323.44'8--dc23
                                                            2013026442

Printed in the United States of America
1 2 3 4 5   18 17 16 15 14

Contents

Chapter 2: Privacy and Technology

Europe's recent proposal for data protection will lead to a legal quagmire and online censorship; therefore, the proposed law should be protested both inside and outside of the European Union.

Chapter 3: Privacy and Sexuality and Reproduction

Chapter 4: Privacy and the Public Interest

Foreword

> *"The problems of all of humanity can only be solved by all of humanity."*
> —*Swiss author Friedrich Dürrenmatt*

Global interdependence has become an undeniable reality. Mass media and technology have increased worldwide access to information and created a society of global citizens. Understanding and navigating this global community is a challenge, requiring a high degree of information literacy and a new level of learning sophistication.

Building on the success of its flagship series, Opposing Viewpoints, Greenhaven Press has created the Global Viewpoints series to examine a broad range of current, often controversial topics of worldwide importance from a variety of international perspectives. Providing students and other readers with the information they need to explore global connections and think critically about worldwide implications, each Global Viewpoints volume offers a panoramic view of a topic of widespread significance.

Drugs, famine, immigration—a broad, international treatment is essential to do justice to social, environmental, health, and political issues such as these. Junior high, high school, and early college students, as well as general readers, can all use Global Viewpoints anthologies to discern the complexities relating to each issue. Readers will be able to examine unique national perspectives while, at the same time, appreciating the interconnectedness that global priorities bring to all nations and cultures.

Material in each volume is selected from a diverse range of sources, including journals, magazines, newspapers, nonfiction books, speeches, government documents, pamphlets, organization newsletters, and position papers. Global Viewpoints is truly global, with material drawn primarily from international sources available in English and secondarily from US sources with extensive international coverage.

Features of each volume in the Global Viewpoints series include:

- An **annotated table of contents** that provides a brief summary of each essay in the volume, including the name of the country or area covered in the essay.

- An **introduction** specific to the volume topic.

- A **world map** to help readers locate the countries or areas covered in the essays.

- For each viewpoint, an **introduction** that contains notes about the author and source of the viewpoint explains why material from the specific country is being presented, summarizes the main points of the viewpoint, and offers three **guided reading questions** to aid in understanding and comprehension.

- **For further discussion** questions that promote critical thinking by asking the reader to compare and contrast aspects of the viewpoints or draw conclusions about perspectives and arguments.

- A worldwide list of **organizations to contact** for readers seeking additional information.

- A **periodical bibliography** for each chapter and a **bibliography of books** on the volume topic to aid in further research.

- A comprehensive **subject index** to offer access to people, places, events, and subjects cited in the text, with the countries covered in the viewpoints highlighted.

Global Viewpoints is designed for a broad spectrum of readers who want to learn more about current events, history, political science, government, international relations, economics, environmental science, world cultures, and sociology—students doing research for class assignments or debates, teachers and faculty seeking to supplement course materials, and others wanting to understand current issues better. By presenting how people in various countries perceive the root causes, current consequences, and proposed solutions to worldwide challenges, Global Viewpoints volumes offer readers opportunities to enhance their global awareness and their knowledge of cultures worldwide.

Juanita High School
10601 NE 132nd St
Kirkland, WA 98034

Introduction

> "No one shall be subjected to arbitrary interference with his privacy, family, home or correspondence, nor to attacks upon his honour and reputation. Everyone has the right to the protection of the law against such interference or attacks."
>
> Article 12, Universal
> Declaration of Human Rights,
> United Nations

National and international debate about the protection of privacy is at a high point. Recent advancements in technology have fueled the debate, raising new challenges and new areas of controversy. Prior to the advent of technology, privacy was largely a matter of being secure in one's home and drawing the curtains. However, new technology related to communications, security, commerce, and medicine has radically altered the privacy landscape, leaving individuals vulnerable to the loss of privacy through the storage and transfer of large amounts of digital information. Various international agreements, regional conventions, and national and state constitutions call for the protection of privacy. But determining how this protection applies in practice is an ongoing challenge on the local, national, and international levels.

Several international agreements protect privacy. Article 12 of the Universal Declaration of Human Rights (UDHR), adopted by the member states of the United Nations (UN) in 1948, declared the right of privacy for individuals. It declared the right to territorial and communications privacy, specifically referring to protection of "privacy, family, home or correspondence," as well as protection from attacks on "honour and reputation." These protections were reiterated in article 17 of the International Covenant on Civil and Political Rights (ICCPR), adopted in 1966. The passage of the UN Convention on the Rights of the Child in 1989 specifically extends those same rights to children in article 16.

Not all countries in the world are part of the United Nations and not all member states directly ratified the UDHR and ICCPR, although both documents had the support of a sufficient number of nations to take effect. For example, among the 193 member states of the United Nations, the ICCPR has 167 states as parties, 74 as signatories and the rest by accession or succession. Whereas the UDHR is simply a declaration, the ICCPR is a treaty with binding commitments. Nonetheless, a number of parties to the ICCPR made reservations or interpretative declarations to their adoption of the covenant. The enforcement of the ICCPR is challenging for this reason and because the language of the covenant is open to interpretation within specific situations affecting individual privacy.

Regional conventions also recognize certain protections for privacy. Article 8 of the European Convention for the Protection of Human Rights and Fundamental Freedoms states that "everyone has the right to respect for his private and family life, his home and his correspondence." Article 11 of the American Convention on Human Rights, ratified by nations of Central America and South America in 1978, reflects the content of the ICCPR: "No one may be the object of arbitrary or abusive interference with his private life, his family, his home, or his correspondence, or of unlawful attacks on his honor or reputation." Article 17 of the Arab Charter on Human Rights, adopted in 1994, says, "Private life is sacred, and violation of that sanctity is a crime. Private life includes family privacy, the sanctity of the home, and the secrecy of correspondence and other forms of private communication." The African Charter on Human and Peoples' Rights, which came into effect in 1986, does not explicitly protect a right to privacy, but article 4 of the African Union Declaration of Principles on Freedom of Expression, adopted in 2002 by the African Commission on Human and Peoples' Rights, guarantees "privacy laws shall not inhibit the dissemination of information of public interest." Additionally, article 10 of the African Charter on the Rights and Welfare of the Child, entered into force in 1999, guarantees certain privacy protections for children: "No child shall be subject to arbitrary or unlawful interference with his privacy, family home or correspondence, or to the attacks upon his honour or reputation."

National and state protections for privacy vary around the world. In the United States, for example, the right to privacy is not explicitly mentioned in the US Constitution but has come to be recognized as a fundamental right of all Americans through laws enacted to protect privacy in specific areas and common law created by court decisions. As in many European countries, libel and slander tort law in the United States protects individual privacy by creating avenues for individuals to sue for damages if privacy is unduly violated. US Supreme Court decisions have cemented the right to privacy in the marital, sexual, and reproductive spheres starting in 1965. The European Union recently passed a directive governing the protection of personal data, offering greater protection for financial data, criminal records, and information collected online. This directive exceeds data protection laws in many other parts of the world, including the United States, creating challenges for implementation given the nature of the Internet.

Although international agreements, regional conventions, and national and state constitutions offer similar broad protections for privacy, the manner in which such protection applies in specific situations is open to debate. With respect to new technologies, there is a lack of consensus regarding how privacy protections apply. Terrorist activities around the world in recent years, combined with new technologies, have led to more surveillance of individuals around the world through cameras, airport security, and the monitoring of communications. This increased invasion of privacy has led to a fiery debate around the world about the appropriate balance between privacy and security. In addition, the collection of information on the Internet by businesses poses completely new challenges to privacy laws that were created before the advent of online communication. These different approaches to protecting privacy in the realm of new technologies around the world are explored through the diverse viewpoints in *Global Viewpoints: Privacy*.

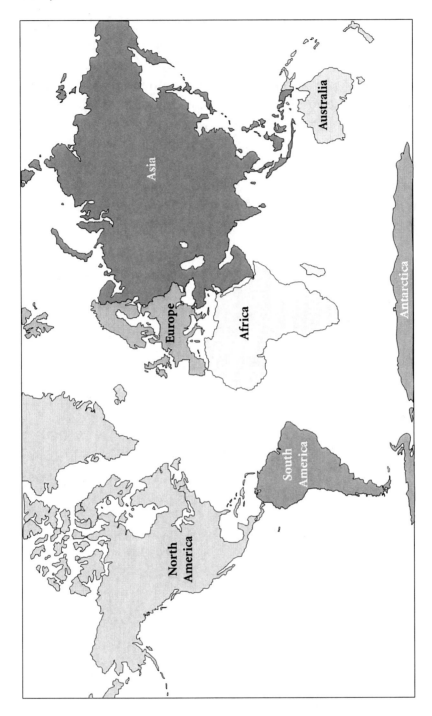

GLOBALVIEWPOINTS

CHAPTER 1

Privacy and Security

Most US Air Travelers OK Sacrificing Privacy for Security: Frequent Travelers Largely OK with Body Scans, More Negative on Pat-Downs

Lymari Morales

In the following viewpoint, Lymari Morales argues that a recent poll shows that most Americans are willing to give up personal privacy to make air travel more secure. Morales claims that frequent air travelers respond more favorably to full-body scans than full-body pat downs, with the majority of people unbothered by scans. Furthermore, she contends that travelers believe that full-body scans are more effective at preventing terrorism. Morales is an adjunct professor of journalism at American University's School of Communication in Washington, DC, and editorial director of Atlantic Media Company.

As you read, consider the following questions:

1. What percentage of air travelers who have flown at least twice in the past year say that preventing acts of terrorism is worth loss of privacy, according to the author?

Lymari Morales, "Most US Air Travelers OK Sacrificing Privacy for Security: Frequent Travelers Largely OK with Body Scans, More Negative on Pat-Downs," Gallup, November 23, 2010. Copyright © 2010 by The Gallup Organization. All rights reserved. Reproduced by permission.

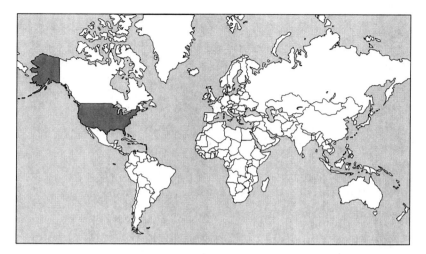

2. According to Morales, what percentage of frequent air travelers would choose a full-body scan over a full-body pat down when going through security?

3. According to the author, what is the Homeland Security Department's rationale for full-body scans and full-body pat downs?

Washington, D.C.—Despite a reported uproar about full-body screening procedures now in broader use at U.S. airports and calls for a boycott, Gallup finds that relatively few frequent U.S. air travelers are angry about the new procedures or inclined to cut back on flying as a result. The large majority (71%) of air travelers who have flown at least twice in the past year say any potential loss of personal privacy from the full-body scans and pat-downs is worth it as a means of preventing acts of terrorism.

The results are from a *USA Today*/Gallup poll conducted Nov. 19–21, 2010, in which 23% of respondents say they have flown two or more times in the past year. The majority of Americans (62%) say they have not flown at all in the past 12 months, and 15% have flown once.

Gallup asked those who have flown two or more times in the past year about the full-body scans and pat-downs the Transportation Security Administration is now using at many U.S. airports as a means to prevent acts of terrorism. The majority (57%) say they are not bothered by the prospect of undergoing a full-body scan at airport security checkpoints. The same percentage, however, say they are bothered, if not angry, about the prospect of undergoing a full-body pat-down. Still, fewer than one in three frequent air travelers are "angry" about undergoing either procedure.

About one in four (24%) frequent travelers Gallup surveyed say they have already undergone a full-body scan this year, and 15% say they have undergone a pat-down. Notably, more than two-thirds of those who had actually undergone the screening say it did not bother them—suggesting that the prospect of the procedure is more bothersome than the reality.

Americans' greater comfort with the body scan procedure over the full-body pat-down is evident, as 75% of frequent air travelers say they would choose a full-body scan over a full-body pat-down when going through security; 22% would choose a pat-down.

The majority (57%) say they are not bothered by the prospect of undergoing a full-body scan at airport security checkpoints.

Regardless of their preferences and whether they had personally undergone one of these procedures, Gallup asked frequent air travelers how effective they perceived these tactics to be at preventing terrorists from smuggling dangerous objects or explosives on board airplanes. Frequent travelers tend to agree that the full-body scans are more effective than other

Views on Loss of Personal Privacy

Consider any loss of personal privacy air travelers may experience from going through a full-body scan or a full-body pat down. Do you think that loss of personal privacy is worth it or not worth it as a method to prevent acts of terrorism?

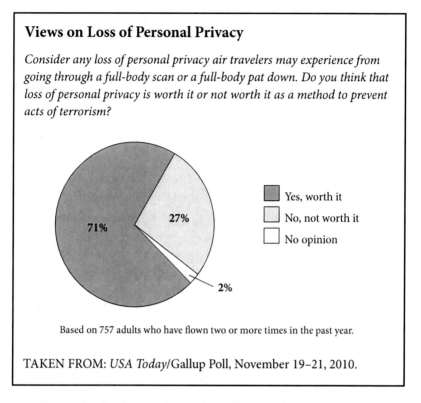

Based on 757 adults who have flown two or more times in the past year.

TAKEN FROM: *USA Today*/Gallup Poll, November 19–21, 2010.

search methods, but are evenly split on the pat-downs. This basic breakdown persists among those who have undergone the procedures.

Overall, relatively few travelers appear fazed enough by the security screenings to change their travel plans. Fewer than 2 in 10 (19%) say they are more likely now than in the past to use alternative means of transportation to avoid the hassles associated with air travel, while 79% say they are just as likely to fly as in the past. These views are no worse than when the increased use of full-body scans began in January.

Implications

Attitudes among frequent U.S. air travelers suggest that the reported uproar over the use of full-body scans and pat-downs at U.S. airports does not reflect how most air travelers feel. The majority are not bothered by the use of full-body scans, which most travelers would choose over the full-body pat-downs they tend to find objectionable and less effective at preventing terrorism. Further, in both cases, those who have already undergone such procedures are less likely to have been bothered or angry than those who have not, suggesting that the prospect of such a screening is more upsetting than the reality.

The large majority of frequent travelers say any potential loss of privacy is worth it to prevent acts of terrorism, which suggests that most Americans accept the Homeland Security Department's rationale for using these tactics. Airlines can also find solace in that air travelers appear no less likely to use other means of travel than they were at the start of the year, when the use of these procedures was less common.

Survey Methods

Results for this *USA Today*/Gallup poll are based on telephone interviews conducted Nov. 19–21, 2010, with a random sample of 3,018 adults, aged 18 and older, living in the continental U.S., selected using random-digit-dial sampling.

For results based on the total sample of national adults, one can say with 95% confidence that the maximum margin of sampling error is ±2 percentage points.

For results based on the sample of 757 frequent air travelers (those who have flown twice or more in the past year), one can say with 95% confidence that the margin of error is ±4 percentage points.

The large majority of frequent travelers say any potential loss of privacy is worth it to prevent acts of terrorism.

Interviews are conducted with respondents on landline telephones (for respondents with a landline telephone) and cellular phones (for respondents who are cell phone–only). Each sample includes a minimum quota of 150 cell phone–

only respondents and 850 landline respondents, with additional minimum quotas among landline respondents for gender within region. Landline respondents are chosen at random within each household on the basis of which member had the most recent birthday.

Samples are weighted by gender, age, race, education, region, and phone lines. Demographic weighting targets are based on the March 2009 Current Population Survey figures for the aged 18 and older non-institutionalized population living in continental U.S. telephone households. All reported margins of sampling error include the computed design effects for weighting and sample design.

In addition to sampling error, question wording and practical difficulties in conducting surveys can introduce error or bias into the findings of public opinion polls.

In the United States, Too Much Privacy Is Being Sacrificed for Security

Daniel J. Solove

In the following viewpoint, Daniel J. Solove argues that in the debate about privacy and security, the victory for security often rests on fallacious arguments. Solove recounts several pro-security arguments—including the all-or-nothing fallacy, the deference argument, the pendulum argument, the war-powers argument, and the Luddite argument—finding flaws with each. Solove is the John Marshall Harlan Research Professor of Law at George Washington University and the author of Nothing to Hide: The False Tradeoff Between Privacy and Security.

As you read, consider the following questions:

1. According to Solove, what wrong question are people usually asked in polls about giving up privacy?
2. The author claims that courts usually side with the government on issues of searches and surveillance, trumping the rights guaranteed by what amendment?
3. What analogy does the author make to support his view that adopting new technologies prematurely can be dangerous?

Daniel J. Solove, "Why 'Security' Keeps Winning Out over Privacy," *Salon*, May 31, 2011. Copyright © 2011 by Salon.com. All rights reserved. Reproduced with permission.

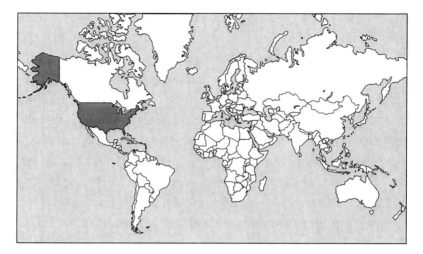

Far too often, debates about privacy and security begin with privacy proponents pointing to invasive government surveillance, such as GPS [global positioning system] tracking, the National Security Agency [NSA] surveillance program, data mining, and public video camera systems. Security proponents then chime in with a cadre of arguments about how these security measures are essential to law enforcement and national security. When the balancing is done, the security side often wins, and security measures go forward with little to no privacy protections.

But the victory for security is one often achieved unfairly. The debate is being skewed by several flawed pro-security arguments. These arguments improperly tip the scales to the security side of the balance. Let's analyze some of these arguments, the reasons they are flawed, and the pernicious effects they have.

The All-or-Nothing Fallacy

Many people contend that "we must give up some of our privacy in order to be more secure." In polls, people are asked whether the government should conduct surveillance if it will help in catching terrorists. Many people readily say yes.

25

But this is the wrong question and the wrong way to balance privacy against security. Rarely does protecting privacy involve totally banning a security measure. It's not all or nothing. Instead, protecting privacy typically means that government surveillance must be subjected to judicial oversight and that the government must justify the need to engage in surveillance. Even a search of our homes is permitted if law enforcement officials obtain a warrant and probable cause. We shouldn't ask: "Do you want the government to engage in surveillance?" Instead, we should ask: "Do you want the government to engage in surveillance without a warrant or probable cause?"

The victory for security is one often achieved unfairly.

We shouldn't be balancing the costs of completely forgoing surveillance against privacy. Instead, the security interest should only be the extent to which oversight and justification will make surveillance less effective. In many cases, privacy protection will not diminish the effectiveness of government security measures all that much. Privacy is losing out in the balance because it is being weighed against completely banning a security measure rather than being balanced against merely making it a little less convenient for the government.

The Deference Argument

Many security proponents argue that courts should defer to the executive branch when it comes to evaluating security measures. In cases where Fourth Amendment rights are pitted against government searches and surveillance, courts often refuse to second-guess the judgment of the government officials. The problem with doing this is that, unless the effectiveness of the security measures is explored, they will win out every time. All the government has to do is mention "terrorism," and whatever it proposes to do in response—whether wise or not—remains unquestioned.

But it is the job of the courts to balance privacy against security, and they can't do this job if they refuse to evaluate whether the security measure is really worth the trade-off. Deference is an abdication of the court's role in ensuring that the government respects constitutional rights. The deference argument is one that impedes any effective balancing of interests.

The Pendulum Argument

In times of crisis, many security proponents claim that we must swing the pendulum toward greater security. "Don't be alarmed," they say. "In peacetime, the pendulum will swing back to privacy and liberty."

The problem with this argument is that it has things exactly backward. During times of crisis, the temptation to make unnecessary sacrifices of privacy and liberty in the name of security is exceedingly high. History has shown that many curtailments of rights were in vain, such as the Japanese American internment during World War II and the McCarthy-era hysteria about Communists [referring to a time in the early 1950s when Senator Joseph McCarthy made public accusations about US citizens and members of government being Communists and Soviet sympathizers]. During times of peace, the need to protect privacy is not as strong because we're less likely to make such needless sacrifices. The greatest need for safeguarding liberty comes during times when we are least inclined to protect it.

The War-Powers Argument

After Sept. 11 [referring to the terrorist attacks on the United States on September 11, 2001], the [George W.] Bush administration authorized the National Security Agency to engage in warrantless wiretapping of the phone calls of Americans.

The Nothing-to-Hide Argument

When the government gathers or analyzes personal information, many people say they're not worried. "I've got nothing to hide," they declare. "Only if you're doing something wrong should you worry, and then you don't deserve to keep it private."

The nothing-to-hide argument pervades discussions about privacy. The data-security expert Bruce Schneier calls it the "most common retort against privacy advocates." The legal scholar Geoffrey Stone refers to it as an "all-too-common refrain." In its most compelling form, it is an argument that the privacy interest is generally minimal, thus making the contest with security concerns a foreordained victory for security.

The nothing-to-hide argument is everywhere. In Britain, for example, the government has installed millions of public surveillance cameras in cities and towns, which are watched by officials via closed-circuit television. In a campaign slogan for the program, the government declares: "If you've got nothing to hide, you've got nothing to fear."

Daniel J. Solove, "Why Privacy Matters Even if You Have 'Nothing to Hide,'" Chronicle Review, *May 15, 2011.*

Headquartered in Maryland, the NSA is the world's largest top-secret spy organization. The NSA surveillance program violated the Foreign Intelligence Surveillance Act (FISA), a federal law that required courts to authorize the kind of wiretapping the NSA engaged in. The Bush administration didn't justify its actions on an argument that it was acting legally under FISA. Instead, it argued that the president had the right to break the law because of the "inherent constitutional authority" of the president to wage war.

The war-powers argument is so broad that it fails of its own weight. If the president's power to wage war encompasses breaking any law that stands in the way, then the president has virtually unlimited power. A hallmark feature of our legal system is the rule of law. We repudiated a monarchy in the American Revolution, and we established a nation where laws would rule, not a lone dictator. The problem with the war-powers argument is that it eviscerates the rule of law. The most unfortunate thing is that Congress responded with a mere grumble, nothing with teeth—and not even teeth were bared. The message is now clear—in times of crisis, the rule of law can be ignored with impunity. That's a terrifying precedent.

The greatest need for safeguarding liberty comes during times when we are least inclined to protect it.

The Luddite Argument

Government officials love new technology, especially new security technologies like biometric identification and the "naked scanners" at the airport. The security industry lobbies nervous government officials by showing them a dazzling new technology and gets them to buy it. Often, these technologies are not fully mature. Security proponents defend the use of these technologies by arguing that privacy proponents are Luddites who are afraid of new technology. But this argument is grossly unfair.

To see the problems with the Luddite argument, let's look at biometrics. Biometric identification allows people to be identified by their physical characteristics—fingerprint, eye pattern, voice and so on. The technology has a lot of promise, but there is a problem, one I call the "*Titanic* phenomenon." The *Titanic* was thought to be unsinkable, so it lacked adequate lifeboats. If biometric data ever got lost, we could be in a *Titanic*-like situation—people's permanent physical characteristics could be in the hands of criminals, and people could never reclaim their identities. Biometric identification depends on information about people's characteristics being stored in a database. And we hear case after case of businesses and government agencies that suffer data security breaches.

We can't have a meaningful balance between privacy and security unless we improve the way we debate the issue.

One virtue of our current clunky system of identification is that if data gets leaked, a person can clean up the mess. If your Social Security number is seized by an identity thief, you can get a new one. For sure, it's a hassle, but you can restore your identity. But what happens if your eye pattern gets into the hands of an identity thief? You can't get new eyes. Given the government's existing track record for data security, I'm not sure I'm ready to risk the government having such critical information about me that could cause such lasting and unfixable harm if lost. This isn't Luddism—it's caution. It is heeding the lessons of the *Titanic*. Security proponents just focus on the benefits of these technologies, but we also must think about what happens if they fail. This doesn't mean not adopting the technologies, but it means we should be cautious.

These are just a few of the flawed arguments that have shaped the privacy/security debate. There are many others, such as the argument made by people who say they have "nothing to hide." We can't have a meaningful balance between privacy and security unless we improve the way we debate the issue. We must confront and weed out the flawed arguments that have been improperly skewing the conversation.

In the United Kingdom, Extensive Video Surveillance Raises Privacy Concerns

Big Brother Watch

In the following viewpoint, Big Brother Watch argues that the ubiquity of closed-circuit television (CCTV) surveillance cameras in the United Kingdom uses large amounts of taxpayer resources without evidence that the cameras are effective at reducing crime. Big Brother Watch claims that privacy concerns have not been adequately addressed and that surveillance by CCTV cameras lacks adequate oversight and study. Big Brother Watch is an organization in the United Kingdom that works to challenge policies that threaten privacy as well as to expose the true scale of the surveillance state.

As you read, consider the following questions:

1. Big Brother Watch cites a 2002 study estimating that there were how many closed-circuit television (CCTV) surveillance cameras in the United Kingdom?

2. The author argues that CCTV cameras should be eliminated if they do not solve a crime for what length of time?

Big Brother Watch, "The Price of Privacy: How Local Authorities Spent £515m on CCTV in Four Years," February 2012. Copyright © 2012 Big Brother Watch. All rights reserved. Republished with permission.

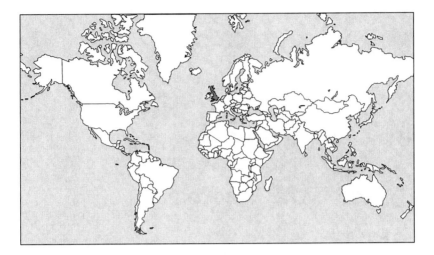

3. Big Brother Watch claims that statements supporting the effectiveness of CCTV cameras are not based on evidence but on what?

The closed-circuit television (CCTV) camera has become a ubiquitous feature on Britain's streets. Hanging from walls, positioned atop lampposts, and hidden behind blacked-out glass, cash-strapped local authorities have spent unprecedented amounts of taxpayers' money making the United Kingdom [UK] the most watched nation of people anywhere in the world. In the past decade alone, the number of CCTV cameras surveying town centre shopping precincts, parks and other public places has increased tenfold.

Some reports have estimated that Britain is home to as many as 20% of the world's total CCTV cameras. One study in 2002 put the total number of CCTV cameras in the UK at around 4.2 million cameras. In London, it is estimated that on average, an individual may be recorded by over 300 different cameras during a single day. The Metropolitan Police's own research found how less than one crime was solved by every 1,000 cameras in the capital. . . .

Misconceptions About CCTV

In the current financial climate, sustaining the level of investment in CCTV is impossible to justify. The surveillance British citizens are now subjected to continues to increase, despite being at a level that makes many other democratic countries recoil in horror.

CCTV does not have a significant deterrent effect on crime, and is not a substitute for police. Yet it continues to be claimed—without evidence—that more CCTV improves public safety.

Big Brother Watch accepts CCTV has a role to play in tackling crime, but the current state of affairs is based not upon evidence but hearsay and conjecture, with reasonable concerns about privacy and civic society brushed aside with little regard.

It is not unreasonable, for example, to ask councils to use crime data to decide on where cameras are positioned, and use non-fixed cameras as part of an operation to tackle the root cause of the problem. However, this will only work if cameras are *part* of the police's action, rather than being used *instead* of police action.

The surveillance British citizens are now subjected to continues to increase, despite being at a level that makes many other democratic countries recoil in horror.

The public's perception of CCTV is based on a widespread misconception that cameras are monitored, and in the event of an incident an operator would be able to send help. This is not true, with the overwhelming majority of cameras only used after an event has been reported—with many either not functioning or able to provide an image of sufficient quality. As a result, the public debate about CCTV has been skewed, something we hope to address.

A Look at the Evidence

There remains little evidence that suggests further investment in CCTV will directly reduce crime, in particular crimes against people. Equally, retaining the current level of surveillance directs resources away from alternatives [that] could have a greater impact on both preventing and solving crime.

The 2007 CCTV strategy recognised how Britain's CCTV infrastructure had been *"developed in a piecemeal fashion with little strategic direction, control or regulation."*

The huge variation between local authorities highlights how this remains the case and we believe is something that urgently requires attention. In the same way that speed cameras cannot be installed on a whim, but require a process of establishing what the root causes of the problem are and the evidential evidence of the scale of the problem, we believe CCTV should be subject to a similar process.

Furthermore, we believe that councils should undertake a review of how their own cameras have been used in recent years and identify those that are not being used either to protect infrastructure or solve crimes. Where the camera has not solved a single crime in the past three years, we believe the camera should be turned off.

Retaining the current level of surveillance directs resources away from alternatives [that] could have a greater impact on both preventing and solving crime.

A Code of Practice

The Protection of Freedoms Bill [officially the Protection of Freedoms Act 2012] proposes a national CCTV code of practice, to be enforced by a national CCTV regulator. This is an important step to properly regulating CCTV and must not be a symbolic gesture.

We believe to restore public faith in CCTV, better inform debate and to strengthen the protections afforded to our privacy, the government should adopt the following five policy objectives.

1. Give the CCTV regulator the powers to enforce the code of practice.

The situation in Oxford and Southampton highlights the ineffectiveness of the current regulatory structure. The Information Commissioner's Office code of practice for CCTV makes clear CCTV should only be used to record video *and audio* in very rare and extreme circumstances. Both these local authorities have decided that as a condition of their license, taxis should record both audio and video, but the only recourse to challenge their policies—in effect to enforce the existing code of practice—is for private citizens to mount a judicial review.

The regulator should have powers to order the cessation of policies that contravene the code of practice, and the power to inspect equipment to ensure it is compliant.

The debate around CCTV lacks any real measurement of effectiveness.

---

2. Any publicly funded CCTV installation should have to refer to crime statistics or demonstrate a significant risk of harm before being commenced.

Prior to installation, this would require councils to publish an evidential basis for camera installation, and also raise strategic questions before a decision has been taken. It would also highlight situations where temporary, non-fixed cameras would be a better solution than inflexible, fixed cameras.

The availability of crime maps enables this to be delivered without significant administrative burdens and would restore trust in the use of CCTV. Where residents suspect that surveillance is designed to, for example, [determine] the number of monetary penalties issued for parking offences, this process would improve transparency and better inform debate.

3. Public bodies should publish the instances where their CCTV cameras have been used in securing a conviction, and for what offences.

This simple statistic would enable the public to see the true impact of CCTV, and ensure that multi-function cameras continue to be used for the reasons stated when they were installed.

The debate around CCTV lacks any real measurement of effectiveness, and despite academic research highlighting the weak deterrent effect of CCTV, statements alluding to the effectiveness of CCTV continue to be made based on personal beliefs instead of evidence.

4. Public bodies should be required (save for those used in direct protection of sites at risk of terrorism) to publish in a standardised format the locations of their cameras.

Despite the advances made in open data and transparency, particularly the publication of crime statistics in crime maps, it is still difficult for any meaningful research to take place around the impact of CCTV on crime. This is largely down to the huge variations between different authorities in both how the location of cameras is recorded and what information is made public.

A simple, standardised location publication scheme would not be a significant administrative burden, as demonstrated by those authorities who already make available the ordinance survey or GPS [global positioning system] location of their cameras. We believe this would then allow people to make an informed decision about whether the level of surveillance is having an impact on crime and to expose the patterns in camera deployment that currently exist.

5. The government should begin a consultation on regulating private CCTV cameras, both those operated by commercial companies and by private individuals.

Clearly, as this research highlights, the overwhelming majority of CCTV cameras are privately operated. However, many of the same issues arise when considering how they are used, the risk of misuse and the wider implications for privacy. Therefore, we believe there needs to be consideration about the wider regulation of private CCTV to address the concerns that exist, and to assist in the development of the code of practice.

Furthermore, the continued growth in private individuals installing CCTV cameras raises new questions not addressed by existing regulation, with private CCTV specifically exempted from the Data Protection Act, for example. The consultation should evaluate the scale of the use of private CCTV and the growing sense of frustration that there is no redress against those abusing their ability to install cameras.

In India, Surveillance for Security Is a Government Privilege, Not a Right

Manasi Kakatkar-Kulkarni

In the following viewpoint, Manasi Kakatkar-Kulkarni argues that recent accusations of wiretapping in India illustrate the need for more pointed legislation governing the right to privacy. Kakatkar-Kulkarni claims that there is indirect protection of privacy within the Indian Constitution but contends that this is not adequate. She claims that recent surveillance by the government needs to be clearly codified as exceptional and that new technology creates the need to revisit privacy protections. Kakatkar-Kulkarni writes for the Foreign Policy Association's blog.

As you read, consider the following questions:

1. According to Kakatkar-Kulkarni, what article of the Indian Constitution indirectly guarantees a right to privacy?

2. Laws that govern phone and wiretapping are found in what piece of legislation, according to the author?

3. Kakatkar-Kulkarni claims that during times of crisis, citizenry grants what privilege to government?

Manasi Kakatkar-Kulkarni, "Essential Surveillance and the Right to Privacy," Foreign Policy Association, April 28, 2010. Copyright © 2010 by Foreign Policy Association. All rights reserved. Reproduced by permission.

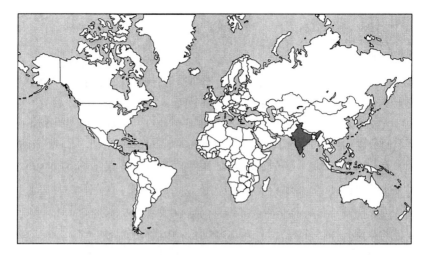

The last few days [in April 2010] have seen significant up-roar in the Indian parliament and media about the alleged wiretapping of four senior politicians in India. The *Outlook* magazine reported that telephones of Bihar chief minister Nitish Kumar, union agriculture minister Sharad Pawar, CPI(M) [Communist Party of India (Marxist)] general secretary Prakash Karat and Congress general secretary Digvijay Singh were tapped by intelligence agencies at various points of time. The opposition parties and the media alleged that the Manmohan Singh government had authorised these wiretappings for political interests. However, the government has categorically denied its involvement in any such action, and set up an inquiry to examine the veracity of the report published in *Outlook*.

The Right to Privacy

Whether the government directly issued orders or if it was a case of accidental random sweep, we might never know; but it sure raises the question of the absence of a direct fundamental right to privacy in the Indian Constitution. Court judgments over the years imply that individual privacy is indirectly guaranteed under [article] 21 which protects the right to life and liberty. Such indirect protection is insufficient in a society where individual space and privacy are culturally very limited. Out of goodwill or sheer nosiness, everyone is into everybody's business. And it is considered impolite to shoo these 'well-wishers' away. It is therefore no surprise that the right to privacy is not enshrined in the Indian Constitution as a fundamental right. Neither are there stringent laws ensuring individual privacy and protection from unwelcome intrusion by individuals or governments.

Indirect protection is insufficient in a society where individual space and privacy are culturally very limited.

Phone/wiretapping laws can be found in the 1885 Indian Telegraph Act, but they fall seriously short of 21C realities. In a 1997 judgment, the Supreme Court of India had "*observed that unlawful means of phone tapping are invasions in privacy and are uncivilized and undemocratic in nature.*" It had issued guidelines to be followed for authorizing wiretappings, but today's advanced technologies can easily circumvent them. As reported by *Outlook* magazine, the National Technical Research Organisation (NTRO), a technical intelligence gathering agency created in 2004, tapped the cell phone of the four leaders using the off-the-air GSM [global system for mobile communications] monitoring device. The device can tap into any conversation within a two kilometer radius without any assistance from the service provider. "*Depending on weather conditions we can detect and intercept a GSM mobile number at least 2 km away even though the number is not available to us. . . . All we have to do is to set up a mobile monitoring system by placing the device in a car and then drive around the likely areas of the phone we want to put under surveillance. Once the call is detected, the device hooks on to the number and continues to track and record calls made or received. Sometimes, we take a voice sample from a TV recording and use it to identify the cell phone if we are monitoring a public figure."*

Other intrusive actions by intelligence and law enforcement agencies require all telecom providers to be part of the surveillance efforts. *"A telephone company has to set up a 20 ft [foot] by 20 ft room with eight computers in every city. . . . Each computer belongs to a designated agency, which can use it to access all data, phone call records and, if necessary, even record calls of a particular number, provided the union or state home secretary has authorised it."*

The Indian parliament . . . should seriously take up the task of legislating the protection of individual privacy.

The Need for Legislative Protection

While the terror situation these days can help rationalize such drastic measures for national security purposes, it also lays the burden on the government to ensure that it does not abuse its powers. The accidental intrusion of individual privacy due to advanced surveillance methods is a privilege the citizenry grants its government in times of crisis. It should not be used as a right. The Indian parliament, instead of engaging in shouting matches and walkouts, should seriously take up the task of legislating the protection of individual privacy. Technological advances are shrinking personal space. But willful shrinking through social networking sites should not be confused with a free run for government agencies to poke around in people's lives. A serious debate in the parliament is necessary to determine whether the right to privacy can be guaranteed as a fundamental right. The 1885 Telegraph Act should be revisited and amended with the current realities in mind. Wiretapping laws need to be made stringent with a competent authority designated to determine and authorise when such wiretapping is critical to national security. It should also include relevant laws for protection of individuals' rights, pri-

Constitutional Protections for Privacy in India

Although the Indian Constitution does not contain an explicit reference to a right to privacy, this right has been read into the Constitution by the Supreme Court as a component of two fundamental rights: the right to freedom under article 19 and the right to life and personal liberty under article 21.

Part III of the Constitution of India (articles 12 through 35) is titled 'Fundamental Rights'; it lists several rights that are regarded as fundamental to all citizens of India (some fundamental rights, notably the right to life and liberty apply to all persons in India, whether they are citizens or not). Article 13 forbids the state from making "any law which takes away or abridges" the fundamental rights.

Article 19(1)(a) stipulates that "all citizens shall have the right to freedom of speech and expression". However, this is qualified by article 19(2) which states that this will not "affect the operation of any existing law, or prevent the state from making any law, in so far as such law imposes reasonable restrictions on the exercise of the right.". . .

Thus the freedom of expression guaranteed by article 19(1)(a) is not absolute, but a qualified right that is susceptible, under the constitutional scheme, to being curtailed under specific conditions.

The other important fundamental right from the perspective of privacy jurisprudence is article 21, which reads: "No person shall be deprived of his life or personal liberty except according to procedure established by law."

Privacy International, "Report India:
Chapter II: Legal Framework," 2013.

vacy and information in the cyber world. With the project for a unique identification number for all Indian citizens under way, it is necessary to incorporate watertight methods for protection of information, identity theft and misuse by persons for malicious purposes.

It is necessary that Indian society learns to recognise and respect individual space and privacy beyond the cultural confines it has stuck to so far. If a person cannot be guaranteed an intrusion-free private life by people around him, it would be wrong to assume that the government will. Essential surveillance is a grey area; the Indian parliament needs to define it.

The Politics of Surveillance: The Erosion of Privacy in Latin America

Katitza Rodríguez

In the following viewpoint, Katitza Rodríguez argues that there have been several recent scandals in Latin America involving illegal government surveillance of communications. Rodríguez points to incidents in Colombia, Peru, Paraguay, and Panama, as well as policies in Brazil and Mexico, in support of her view that citizens' privacy rights in Latin America are under attack. Additionally, she claims that US Drug Enforcement Administration (DEA) surveillance technology is in danger of being misused in Latin America. Rodríguez is international rights director for the Electronic Frontier Foundation.

As you read, consider the following questions:

1. According to the author, the most severe instance of recent widespread government surveillance in Latin America took place in what country?
2. What country repeatedly requested technical assistance from the United States to extend its wiretapping capacity, according to Rodríguez?

Katitza Rodríguez, "The Politics of Surveillance: The Erosion of Privacy in Latin America," *Index on Censorship*, vol. 40, no. 2, April 2011, pp. 116–123. Copyright © 2011 Index on Censorship. All rights reserved. Republished with permission.

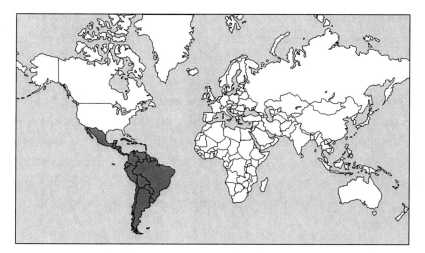

3. According to the author, what are citizens in Mexico required to provide to obtain a mobile phone number?

Political opponents and activists are among those monitored in Latin America. Katitza Rodríguez charts the erosion of privacy in the region.

While most Latin American countries have democratically elected governments, many still fail to respect human rights, including the right to privacy. Across the region, there have been multiple scandals involving government officials and intelligence agencies engaged in illegal surveillance of communications. These include numerous chilling examples of how interception technologies are being misused to spy on politicians, dissidents, judges, human rights organizations and activists. Although privacy violations vary from country to country, and the full extent of government surveillance in the region remains largely unknown, newly disclosed data-gathering programs hint at the architecture of surveillance lying beneath the surface of ostensibly democratic societies.

These surveillance systems demonstrate how communication interception is being used as a political tool to identify, control and stifle dissent. Their use also highlights the lack of transparency and accountability that surrounds pervasive government surveillance in many Latin American countries. In 2009, Colombia's 'Las Chuzadas' scandal revealed that members of the country's intelligence service allegedly carried out illegal, widespread surveillance and wiretapping of key politicians, judges, dissidents and human rights NGOs. Litigation about the surveillance is currently pending in the Colombian courts. In March 2011, the Inter-American Commission on Human Rights opened an investigation into the role of Colombian state officials in executing this mass surveillance programme.

Perhaps the most severe instance of widespread government surveillance took place in Peru during the presidency of Alberto Fujimori. Fujimori, who is currently in jail, was convicted of mass illegal surveillance of prominent Peruvian citizens. Peruvian prosecutors found that the former president devised and implemented 'Plan Emilio' to conduct nationwide surveillance of politicians, ministers, journalists and activists. In 2010, judicial authorities in Peru discovered a former naval intelligence employee illegally intercepted 52,947 emails from journalists and political opponents of the Fujimori government between 1999 and 2000. The case has yet to go to court.

Across the region, there have been multiple scandals involving government officials and intelligence agencies engaged in illegal surveillance of communications.

Leaked US diplomatic cables posted on the WikiLeaks whistleblower website shed light on the US Drug Enforcement Administration's (DEA) communications surveillance programme and how the governments of Paraguay and Panama pressured the US government to allow the use of these technologies for operations unrelated to narcotics investigations. According to the cables, both countries sought US cooperation to expand their respective capacities to spy on mobile communications for political gain.

In Paraguay, this surveillance was undertaken ostensibly to deal with the threat of the leftist guerrilla group the Paraguayan People's Army. A diplomatic cable dated 18 February 2010 reveals that the DEA conducted an active mobile phone spying programme for counter-narcotics efforts in Paraguay beginning in 2009. The cables also reveal that the Paraguayan government requested access to the software used by the DEA to perform eavesdropping for other purposes. US diplomats even warned about the possibility that these surveillance technologies could be misused for unrestricted eavesdropping and political advantage:

> The ambassador made clear that the US had no interest in involving itself in the intercept programme if the potential existed for it to be abused for political gain, but confirmed US interest in cooperating on an intercept programme with safeguards, as long as it included counter-narcotics. While noting that the interior ministry's current personnel are trustworthy, the ambassador noted that others could abuse this technology in the future.

The US embassy repeatedly denied Paraguayan government requests for unrestricted access to its surveillance software. According to the US envoy, the interior minister of Paraguay disclosed that his government's 'top priority was capturing the [Paraguayan People's Army], which had to take precedence over counter-narcotics'. 'Counter-narcotics are important,' he said, 'but won't topple our government. The [Paraguayan People's Army] could.'

The cables also reveal the nature of 'cooperation' between US law enforcement and Paraguayan telecom companies, illustrating how the US influenced otherwise hesitant actors:

> TIGO (Millicom), one of Paraguay's leading cell phone providers, told the ambassador that though they had concerns

about the [government of Paraguay's] decision to move forward with an intercept programme, they felt that US involvement in the programme would provide them with some 'cover'.

Despite their misgivings, US embassy staff concluded that they could not refuse to cooperate indefinitely without threatening the DEA's broader agenda. 'Get on board or get left behind,' reads the subtitle of the cable. 'If we are not supportive,' the cable continues, 'the [government of Paraguay] will view us as an obstacle to a key priority, which could jeopardise our broader relationship and the DEA's ability to pursue counter-narcotics leads. . . . We have carefully navigated this very sensitive and politically sticky situation, and hope that we can move forward quickly in order to make the most of it.' In effect, the US government acknowledged its surveillance assistance would likely be misused for political surveillance, but continued to cooperate.

A similar dynamic played out in Panama. According to a leaked cable dated 22 August 2009, 'Panama 000639', the Panamanian government, headed by President Ricardo Martinelli, repeatedly requested technical assistance from the US to extend its wiretapping capacity. In July 2009, Martinelli sent a BlackBerry message to the ambassador that read, 'I need help with tapping phones.' Moreover, Martinelli sought the DEA's cooperation to acquire US government support for his politically driven wiretap project. As embassy staff report in the cables, Martinelli thought it was unfair that the 'DEA collects information but that Panama does not benefit from that information'. In his communication with the embassy, he made reference to various groups and individuals he thought should be wiretapped and 'he clearly made no distinction between legitimate security targets and political enemies'. Martinelli went on to say that the US government 'should give the [government of Panama] its own independent wiretap capability as "rent" in exchange for the use of [its] facilities'.

When the Panamanian government threatened to reduce its cooperation with the counter-narcotics surveillance programme, the US ambassador to Panama counter-threatened to inform his superiors in Washington, DC: 'The ambassador forcefully defended the DEA program and pointed out that the jointly investigated cases were taking criminals off of Panama's streets and making the country safer. . . . She would readily inform Washington [of his threat] and [everyone would see] Panama's reputation as a reliable partner plummet dramatically.'

In effect, the US government acknowledged its surveillance assistance would likely be misused for political surveillance, but continued to cooperate.

Although Martinelli backed off, the Panamanian government subsequently confirmed that it could expand the wiretapping programme on its own, and had already met with the heads of Panama's four mobile phone operators to discuss methods for obtaining mobile call data. The US ambassador encouraged the Panamanian government to 'streamline' its process for obtaining emergency court orders for lawful interception, but expressed concerns in another cable about political pressure undermining the independence of the judiciary. According to the cables, Martinelli 'chided' the ambassador's advice for being 'too legal'.

US government officials defended their own wiretap programme in the cables, stating, '[it] works well and upholds the rule of law [and] would easily withstand public scrutiny were it to come to light'. In its coordination with Panamanian authorities to meet US government collection requirements, officials cautioned 'against the danger of local officials trying to commandeer the program for internal political games' and attempted to 'only conduct limited law enforcement wiretap programs in cooperation with Panamanian law enforcement and judicial authorities, directed only against genuine law enforcement targets, in a process managed by a Panamanian prosecutor and approved by a Panamanian supreme court judge'. The effectiveness of legal safeguards against interception of communications depends on government compliance with national law. This disclosure shows why we cannot assume that governments will always comply.

Another cable, dated 24 December 2009, reveals that the US decision to remove the DEA's Matador wiretap programme from Panamanian government control was met with resistance and more threats, citing 'a series of obstacles, including threats from the council for public security and national defense director to expel the DEA from Panama and restrict payments to vetted units and generally weak support for the move from Martinelli and senior [government] leaders'. The US ambassador added that the embassy remained concerned about ongoing efforts by the Panamanian government to weaken judicial controls over domestic surveillance and undermine civil liberties at a time when Panama's judicial institutions were under assault by the executive branch.

'With Panama's notoriously corrupt judicial system (rated 103 out of 133 by the World Economic Forum),' it stated, 'We are not confident that the new judge will uphold the same standards and civil liberties protections that the Panama supreme court has exercised in its oversight of Matador to date.' The ambassador warned his colleagues that the DEA surveillance system should not be used to compromise democratic values in the name of security.

The ambassador concluded by urging the US government not to get entangled in politically motivated wiretapping, advising against involvement in 'questionable activities' in Panama. 'The recent [Las Chuzadas] scandal in Colombia illustrates the catastrophic consequences of politically motivated wiretaps,' he wrote, 'and such a scenario could easily unfold in Panama if the government of Paraguay continues its present course of action. If we cannot guarantee with a high level of confidence that the Matador program will not be misused for political purposes, then we prefer to suspend the program.' Clearly, the ambassador understood the potential dangers posed by the misuse of DEA surveillance systems and how they could be used to undermine free expression and other democratic principles promoted by US policy.

In several countries, there is an emerging trend towards eliminating anonymous communication.

State surveillance can also be achieved through real name registration requirements for the purchase of a mobile phone or SIM card activation. In several countries, there is an emerging trend towards eliminating anonymous communication. Peru, Brazil and Mexico have adopted regulations that compel telecommunications companies to collect and identify prepaid mobile users' contact information for later potential use by law enforcement entities. A similar bill is being discussed in Guatemala. These measures seek to facilitate the identification of criminals and address the alleged threat to security created by the type of mobile phone account that does not require registration or the collection of detailed personal information.

These registration regimes strike a heavy blow against anonymous communications; citizens not suspected of any crime are denied the use of anonymous prepaid cell phones to communicate. In some countries like Peru and Brazil, these identification requirements have been extended to cyber cafes, the medium in which a significant proportion of the population with low incomes accesses the Internet.

To obtain a mobile phone number in Mexico, citizens are required to provide proof of their current address, present the unique identity code given to both citizens and residents of Mexico, produce valid photo identification, and submit to fingerprint scanning. In accordance with the law, Mexican mobile phone companies are responsible for encouraging the users of their 80m devices to register with the National Registry of Mobile Phone Users. In April 2011, Salvador Guerrero, an authority at the Institute for Access to Public Information, criticised the National Registry of Mobile Phone Users for failing to protect the personal data of Mexican citizens: 'During the past year it has become clear that the [registry] is not capable of complying with the function for which it was designed and that is to prevent extortion and kidnapping, the latter figure increasing by eight per cent in 2010 compared to 2009.'

In a few countries, registration requirements are being extended beyond mobiles to Internet cafes. In Peru, Internet cafes are compelled to register the users of their facilities. Brazil adopted a similar measure in April 2011. The sponsor of the Brazilian legislation, Representative Alex Sandro, said of the measure, 'It will be like the prepaid phone, which established a registry for the purchase [of prepaid phones], and the crimes that were committed on these devices still exist, but will decrease greatly because of the possibility of screening.' But this mandate violates the right to speak anonymously, and hinders its crucial function in people's political and social discourse.

A serious discussion is needed about the policy implications of covert surveillance programmes in Latin America and their impact on citizens' privacy and freedom of expression rights.

People should be able to use the Internet anonymously to share sensitive information and express unpopular or controversial opinions without fear of retaliation. The tendency to associate anonymity with criminality by some government officials and law enforcement agencies is troubling. Anonymity is necessary for citizens engaged in legitimate opposition to government policies and for whistleblowers who leak information that those in power would prefer to erase. It is also critical for victims of violence, those who have experienced discrimination because of HIV/AIDS, dissidents, homosexuals and survivors of abuse.

Almost all Latin American countries protect the right to privacy in their constitutions, and a number of countries have signed and/or ratified the UN International Covenant on Civil and Political Rights. But many countries have not yet enacted comprehensive legislation to protect individuals' personal data, with the exception of Argentina, Mexico, Chile and Uruguay. Others (including Brazil, Bolivia, Colombia, Costa Rica, Guatemala and Peru) are currently considering enacting a comprehensive data protection law, or are updating their weak legal safeguards, as in the case of Chile. Governments' demands for the collection and storage of more information, including biometric data in national identification cards or passports, jeopardises individuals' privacy and security, creating a database that has the potential to locate and track people with a high degree of accuracy. Plans for these sorts of databases are currently under way in several countries. A serious discussion is needed about the policy implications of covert surveillance programmes in Latin America and their impact on citizens' privacy and freedom of expression rights.

In Israel, Attitudes About Privacy Are Shaped by Security Concerns

Steven C. Bennett

In the following viewpoint, Steven C. Bennett argues that Israelis have a unique perspective on privacy and the necessary trade-off with security. Bennett claims that privacy policy and legislation in Israel are influenced by Jewish scripture, which holds personal privacy in high regard. The author claims that the unique national security concerns in Israel have created a tolerance for giving up privacy in the name of security. Nonetheless, Bennett claims that there is still concern for privacy, especially as it relates to new technology. Bennett is a partner in the New York law offices of Jones Day.

As you read, consider the following questions:

1. What is the name of the first Jewish justice of the Supreme Court, whose views the author discusses?

2. What law did Israel adopt in 1992 that upholds the right to privacy, according to Bennett?

3. What historical event makes Israelis nervous about the privacy implications of certain information databases, according to the author?

Steven C. Bennett, "Israeli Attitudes on Privacy," *Privacy Advisor*, vol. 9, no. 9, October 2009, pp. 1, 3–5. Copyright © 2009 by Steven C. Bennett. All rights reserved. Republished with permission.

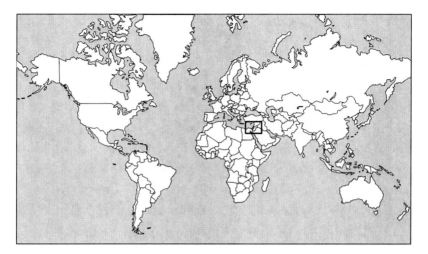

Recently, I had the opportunity to teach a short course on data security and privacy at an Israeli law school. The experience was enlightening.

Israel is a democracy with a highly educated, largely cosmopolitan population. It shares close ties with the United States. Yet, Israel faces unique problems of security, and religious and ethnic tensions are palpable. Israel's legal system, moreover, embodies a unique combination of secular and religious law, with strands of precedent and procedure from many different traditions. The result is a special blend of attitudes on privacy that can only be called "Israeli."

Jewish Views on Privacy

Jewish scripture has long placed a special emphasis on certain aspects of privacy. One passage refers to the "tents of Israel" in ancient times, and suggests that the openings of tents were deliberately kept from facing each other. From this simple tale, the rabbinic scholars derived a sense of the importance of privacy in the home. Jewish law, for example, forbids a neighbor to open a window on a courtyard (without consent), to guard the privacy of a residence. Jewish law also prizes the confidentiality of correspondence and conversation, strictly forbidding a stranger to read a person's private letters, and banning eavesdropping.

It was these Jewish views of privacy that Rabbi Shlomo Yaffe, dean of the Institute of American [and] Talmudic Law, recently cited at a program in New York where U.S. Supreme Court justice Antonin Scalia opined that people with nothing to hide should not be concerned about privacy. "Every single datum about my life is private? That's silly," the justice suggested. Some weeks later, the justice took great offense on learning that a law professor teaching a privacy course had instructed his students to create a dossier on Justice Scalia's most private affairs. The students, with no special skills or assistance, assembled from readily available sources 15 pages of details about Justice Scalia's private life, including his home address and telephone number, his wife's personal email address, photographs of his grandchildren, and the names of TV shows and meals that he prefers. Scalia called the exercise "irresponsible" and "abominably poor judgment," though "legal."

Jewish scripture has long placed a special emphasis on certain aspects of privacy.

The Jewish view of privacy seems to agree with Justice Scalia's later statement of outrage at the exposure of his private affairs. Indeed, Justice Louis Brandeis, the first Jewish justice of the Supreme Court, while still a lawyer, famously wrote in the *Harvard Law Review* (1890) on the "Right to Privacy," a "right to be let alone." Echoing (although not expressly citing) Jewish sources on the importance of the separation of public and private life, Brandeis remarked that the law "secures to each individual the right of determining, ordinarily, to what extent his thoughts, sentiments, and emotions shall be communicated to others." Brandeis worried that "recent inventions and business methods (including the telephone and instant photography) could "invade the sacred precincts of private and domestic life."

The Brandeis View of Privacy

The Brandeis view of privacy did not immediately take hold in American law. In 1928, while on the Supreme Court, Brandeis failed to convince the court that wiretapping of telephone conversations was unconstitutional. In dissent, Brandeis lamented that privacy, "the right most valued by civilized men," could be lost through modern technologies.

Eventually, the Brandeis concern for privacy was enshrined in American constitutional and tort law. In 1967, for example, the Supreme Court ruled that wiretapping without court order was, indeed, a violation of the Fourth Amendment. And, over the course of the twentieth century, U.S. courts increasingly ruled that exposure of intimate details of a person's life, misuse of a person's photograph for commercial gain, and other intrusions could justify relief. Recently, in New York, for example, Woody Allen obtained a multimillion-dollar settlement from a company that used a picture of him dressed as a Hasidic Jew from the movie *Annie Hall*, without his consent.

Thus, the Brandeis view of privacy, nourished and crossbred in the American garden of common law, has grown into a broad (though still somewhat vague) "right of privacy." The Jewish influences and origins of that right, also somewhat obscured, nevertheless can be traced. But what happens when those Jewish seeds are repotted in another country and time?

Modern Israel and the Right to Privacy

Since 1948, Israel has grown quickly, from an agrarian, mostly small-town culture, to a modern, increasingly urban, and technologically astute society. Still, there are certain features of Israeli culture that remain rooted in traditional values.

"Jews have always lived together in close quarters," says one law professor. "They know everything about each other."

A student echoes the sentiment: "In Israel, between every two people who don't know each other, there is always one who can connect them."

On the other hand, in enforcing Jewish values regarding privacy, the close, communal nature of Israeli society may offer some benefits. More than 900 years ago, Rabbi Gershom (a famous Jewish scholar in Germany) introduced the concept of a "cherem," a community boycott applied against those who wrongly read the private letters of their neighbors. This form of community pressure, one student suggests, may still work: "It may be more effective to deal with what is a community issue, in breaches of privacy, with communal tools."

There are certain features of Israeli culture that remain rooted in traditional values.

Even the army, a near-universal experience for Israeli citizens, offers a mix of experiences that may inform Israeli attitudes on privacy. "What privacy?" one student asks. "The government knows everything about us from the day we join the army." On the other hand, the army is a key element in community building. As one older lawyer explains, recruits may form lifetime bonds in their units. Their annual reserve service, moreover, reinforces those bonds, as a sort of "retreat" from daily business concerns.

Israeli Privacy Law

The aim of the law, says one student, is to "design a fair and right society," with people who can "develop and think freely." Despite these lofty aspirations, Israel has never settled on a single, complete, formal constitution. Instead, over a lengthy period, the Knesset (legislature) has adopted a series of "basic" laws, establishing the essential structures of government, and outlining fundamental rights.

In 1992, Israel adopted a basic law on human freedom and dignity, which, among other things, recognized that "all persons have the right to privacy and to intimacy." The basic law, in a classic restatement of Jewish concerns for private life, declares: "There shall be no entry into the private premises of a person who has not consented thereto," and "there shall be no violation of the confidentiality of the spoken utterances, writings, or records of a person." A secret monitoring law, moreover, specifically precludes "listening in" (wiretapping) conversations without consent or court order, and a separate protection of privacy law requires registration of mass databases with a central government authority.

In 1998, moreover, Israel adopted a freedom of information law. And the Israeli Supreme Court has enforced the principle of openness in government, requiring (in one famous case) that Knesset members reveal the terms of the coalition agreements they sign.

Concern About Privacy Protection

Despite these basic laws, a recent report of government and academic experts . . . suggested that Israeli data privacy law requires stepped-up civil (and even criminal) law enforcement efforts. The report criticized administrative regulation of privacy, and recommended some form of class-action device to aggregate small privacy claims that might otherwise escape judicial attention. The report also suggested development of a data breach notification law to ensure that individual citizens are made aware of compromises of their personal data.

Partially in the wake of these reform concerns, the Israeli Law, Information and Technology Authority (ILITA), an agency within the Justice Ministry, recently commenced operations. Although small (with a staff of less than 10) the authority is growing in influence. A recent ILITA conference featured a large and lively audience intent on debating the best means to improve Israeli data protection and privacy.

In December 2008, moreover, Israel's new anti-SPAM law went into effect. The law, consistent with European practice, adopts an "opt-in" approach to commercial messages. Consumers must affirmatively choose to receive advertising. Advertisers who violate the law are subject to serious fines.

Israelis well know the forces arrayed against them and the real risks of terrorism.

National Security Concerns

"We are living in a police state. You must get used to that fact," said an American-born Israeli lawyer over dinner in Jerusalem. "The need for security is paramount." A student emphasized that "when it comes to fighting terrorism," a person "has to trust someone," and "it might as well be your own government." Another law professor went further: "Privacy is a liberal Western concept. It is not part of the Middle East. Besides," she said, "it is 'survival first' here."

In Israel, says one student, "security" is almost a "religious, holy" word. Israelis well know the forces arrayed against them and the real risks of terrorism. Tzipi Livni, then foreign minister of Israel, warned the United Nations in October 2007 of a "global battle" with extremists in which Israel was "on the front lines." Israel, she said, faces daily suicide bombers, rocket attacks, and more.

Tensions have only increased since then, with the election of a more right-oriented Likud coalition government, led by Benjamin Netanyahu. During the election campaign, Netanyahu suggested that the Israeli incursion into Gaza did not go far enough, and that "extremists" would continue wherever Israel relinquished control.

Concern for Personal Freedom

In this highly charged atmosphere, one might expect some imbalance in Israeli views on the trade-off between security and privacy. Yet, the imbalance is moderated by genuine concern for personal freedom. In the classroom, for example, students vigorously debate the issue. "They are experts," says one student, referring to security personnel. "Not like the Americans bumbling at their airports." His classmate disagrees, suggesting that those in charge of the most sensitive information "may not always be qualified or experienced enough." Besides, she says, there is too great a temptation to target those who speak or look Arabic: "It's discrimination," she concludes.

And the consequences can be harrowing. One student told a frightening tale about a drive to Be'er Sheva. Suddenly, his vehicle was surrounded by army scouts with rifles pointed directly at him. They checked his identification and let him go with a brief explanation that he was driving a car that resembled one mentioned in a terrorist alert. Others in the class murmured that this scene is not unique. The pervasive sense of surveillance, they said, can be unsettling.

New technologies, moreover, increase the prospects for surveillance and government data control. Pending before the Knesset, for example, is a bill to create a biometric registry, including fingerprints and digital photographs, for use in all Israeli identification cards and passports. The system would create a national database, registering information on all citizens and residents. A similar system is already in use at certain Palestinian border crossings, and at the Ben Gurion Airport.

Concerns about such systems evoke deep-seated memories. Given the history of the Holocaust, "there is a very uncomfortable sensation of the moral implications of such a [biometric] database," writes one student. Indeed, the head of the Israeli Bar Association committee on privacy law severely criticized the database, noting the risk that it could be hacked by data criminals, or even terrorists. Further, he said, the "government will make potential criminals out of every law-abiding citizen." Another law professor (and advisor to the ILITA) suggests that there is no real security need for the da-

Juanita High School
10801 NE 132nd St
Kirkland, WA 98034

tabase. The Israeli Security Agency, he said, already has sufficient information regarding real security threats (versus the mass of citizens who would become subjects of the database). Yet, the effort has strong support in the Knesset, and may be adopted this year [2009].

Israelis, much like Europeans, largely depend upon their government for security and welfare in ways that may seem excessive to Americans.

Future Directions for Israel

There are very few degrees of separation between Israelis and Americans. Israelis embrace American fashions, language, and business customs. Yet, in the privacy arena, Israel has much more in common with Europe than the U.S. The European Union [EU] has adopted more comprehensive and stringent directives on privacy protection than has the United States. The Europeans, moreover, set the "tone" for Israeli views on privacy regulation. Israel has worked hard in recent years to convince European regulators that its privacy-protection system is "adequate"—a term of significance in European regulation. Yet, the European Union may be influenced by the politics that so pervade all foreign relations with Israel. "We were told by the EU: 'When you stop killing kids in Gaza, we will certify you,'" said one advisor to Israel's mission to the EU.

Still, the parallels to Europe will almost certainly persist. Despite the Holocaust experience, Israelis, much like Europeans, largely depend upon their government for security and welfare in ways that may seem excessive to Americans. Israelis did not suffer through [former U.S. president Lyndon] Johnson and Vietnam or [former U.S. president Richard] Nixon and Watergate. And, in an inversion of [comic strip character] Pogo, "they have met the government and it is us." Thus Israelis, like Europeans, may spend more time fretting about unnecessary interference with consumer and employee privacy, and much less time worrying about the government.

Periodical and Internet Sources Bibliography

The following articles have been selected to supplement the diverse views presented in this chapter.

Julia Angwin	"U.S. Terrorism Agency to Tap a Vast Database of Citizens," *Wall Street Journal*, December 13, 2012.
Ronald Bailey	"Your Cellphone Is Spying on You," *Reason*, January 2013.
Conor Friedersdorf	"The Dangerous, False Trade-Off Between Liberty and Security," *Atlantic*, August 23, 2012.
Human Rights Watch	"'The Root of Humiliation': Abusive Identity Checks in France," January 26, 2012.
Susan Landau	"Surveillance and Security: Securing Whom? And at What Cost?," Privacy International, November 30, 2011. www.privacyinternational.org.
Leesha McKenny	"Council CCTV Use May Break Privacy Law," *Sydney Morning Herald* (Australia), October 17, 2012.
John Naughton	"Airport Scanning Technology Is a Transparent Victory for Terrorism," *Observer* (UK), July 14, 2012.
Paul Pillar	"Poorly Learned Lessons About Terrorism," *National Interest*, October 25, 2012.
Henry Porter	"Hi-Def CCTV Technology Threatens Our Democracy—We Must Act Now," *Guardian* (UK), October 3, 2012.
Naomi Wolf	"The New Totalitarianism of Surveillance Technology," *Guardian* (UK), August 15, 2012.

GLOBALVIEWPOINTS

Privacy and Technology

Private Data, Public Rules

Economist

In the following viewpoint, the Economist *argues that data protection regulations around the world vary widely. The author claims that Europe's new privacy directive is stricter than American standards of privacy, posing a conundrum for companies that have a presence in both places. Additionally, the author contends that privacy legislation likely to come out of China and India will be very different than restrictions seen in the European Union and the United States, further complicating the development of a single data protection regime. The* Economist *is a global newspaper of analysis and opinion.*

As you read, consider the following questions:

1. According to the author, the European Union's justice commissioner claims that its new privacy regulation will save business how much money per year?
2. What percentage of Europeans do not trust Internet companies to protect their personal information, according to the author?
3. According to the author, are the future privacy regulations of China and India likely to be more stringent or less stringent than those of the European Union?

Economist, "Private Data, Public Rules," January 28, 2012. Copyright © 2012 by the Economist Newspaper Ltd. Reproduced by permission.

The world's biggest Internet markets are planning laws to protect personal data. But their approaches differ wildly.

First came the yodelling, then the pain. The online entrepreneurs and venture capitalists at DLD, a geeks' shindig this month in Munich, barely had time to recover from their traditional Bavarian entertainment before Viviane Reding, the European Union's justice commissioner, introduced a new privacy regulation. Ms Reding termed personal data the "currency" of the digital economy. "And like any currency it needs stability and trust," Ms Reding told the assembled digerati.

The EU's effort (formally published on January 25th) is part of a global government crackdown on the commercial use of personal information. A White House report, out soon, is expected to advocate a consumer-privacy law. China has issued several draft guidelines on the issue and India has a privacy bill in the works. But their approaches differ dramatically. As data whizz across borders, creating workable rules for business out of varying national standards will be hard.

Europe's new privacy regulation is one of the most sweeping. Its first goal is to build a "digital single market". That will be a welcome change from the patchwork of rules that has grown up since the previous privacy directive in 1995. When Google's Street View mapping service accidentally captured personal data from some open, unsecured Wi-Fi networks in the houses it photographed, some EU countries told the firm to delete the data. Others told it to hold the information indefinitely.

The commission hopes that when the new regulation comes into effect (probably in 2016) it will clear up this mess. A firm based in, say, Ireland will be able to obey Irish law and do business across the EU, without worrying whether it is in line with other countries' rules. A new European Data Protection Board will enforce the regime. And if a company faces judicial proceedings in two member states, the courts will be obliged to communicate. Ms Reding expects these changes to save business €2.3 billion ($3 billion) a year.

But the new regime is tougher as well as being uniform. Firms must gain proper consent (defined strictly) before using and processing data. They may collect no more information than is necessary and keep it only while they need it. Children's data gain extra safeguards. Users must be able to move information from one service provider to another (for example, an address book between two social networks).

As data whizz across borders, creating workable rules for business out of varying national standards will be hard.

The EU's 500m residents will also win a brand-new right: to be forgotten. Users can not only request that a company show what data it holds on them; they can also demand that it deletes all copies. Critics say this is impractical, vague, and overambitious. It is hard to say where one man's data end and another's begin. And once something is online, it is virtually impossible to ensure that all copies are deleted. Small firms will struggle; even big ones will find the planned penalties steep.

Even more contentiously, the directive covers any firm that does business with Europeans, even if it is based outside the EU. America's Department of Commerce sent the commission a strong 15-page protest, saying that the directive "could hinder commercial interoperability while unintentionally diminishing consumer privacy protection".

An Ocean of Data

That stance reflects differences in American and European attitudes towards data protection, and indeed to regulation in general. America has avoided overly prescriptive privacy legislation, believing that companies should generally regulate themselves. Only when firms fail at self-regulation does the

Federal Trade Commission (FTC) step in. It has broad powers to tackle unfair and deceptive practices, and has not hesitated to use them. In recent rulings, Google and Facebook agreed to a biennial audit of their privacy policies and practices for the next 20 years.

European sensitivities are different. A Eurobarometer poll last year found that 62% of Europeans do not trust Internet companies to protect their personal information. A big reason is history. In the 1930s Dutch officials compiled an impressive national registry. This later enabled the Nazis to identify 73% of Dutch Jews, compared with just 25% in less efficient France, notes Viktor Mayer-Schönberger of Oxford University in his book *Delete: The Virtue of Forgetting in the Digital Age*.

For the global digital economy, differences in privacy laws are a kind of trade barrier and a costly brake on innovation. In the past, Europe and America reached a compromise with the "safe harbour" framework of 2000. As long as American companies adhered to certain principles based on the 1995 directive, they could do business in the EU.

America has avoided overly prescriptive privacy legislation, believing that companies should generally regulate themselves.

The arrangement has worked well, but America now worries that when its new rules come in the EU may want to rejig the deal. America might have more bargaining power if it had its own privacy law on the statute books, some experts argue; in any case public concern about data protection is growing there. On January 24th Google triggered an outcry when it announced that from March it will share data gleaned from people logged into any of its services with all of its businesses, whether those users like it or not.

The administration is hurrying to catch up. In its report, the White House will recommend a legal framework for pri-

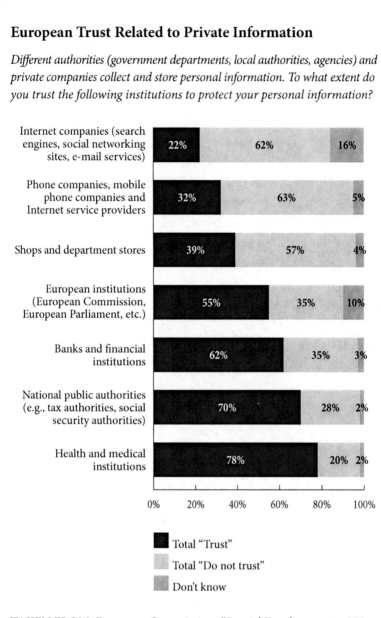

European Trust Related to Private Information

Different authorities (government departments, local authorities, agencies) and private companies collect and store personal information. To what extent do you trust the following institutions to protect your personal information?

Internet companies (search engines, social networking sites, e-mail services): 22%, 62%, 16%

Phone companies, mobile phone companies and Internet service providers: 32%, 63%, 5%

Shops and department stores: 39%, 57%, 4%

European institutions (European Commission, European Parliament, etc.): 55%, 35%, 10%

Banks and financial institutions: 62%, 35%, 3%

National public authorities (e.g., tax authorities, social security authorities): 70%, 28%, 2%

Health and medical institutions: 78%, 20%, 2%

- Total "Trust"
- Total "Do not trust"
- Don't know

TAKEN FROM: European Commission, "Special Eurobarometer 359: Attitudes on Data Protection and Electronic Identity in the European Union," June 2011.

vacy, plus new codes of conduct. The chances of legislation passing in an election year are slim, even on what is usually a bipartisan issue. Talks among business lobbies, privacy activists and regulators may at least produce non-statutory codes, though without the imminent threat of legislation some companies may dawdle.

America and Europe will set the global standards. But other countries' privacy rules matter too.

The FTC will also release a privacy report later this year. This will look broadly at the use of personal data being scooped up by companies on- and offline. Among other things, it is likely to applaud progress in letting Internet users take steps to block tracking by tweaking their web browsers. It will probably support a tougher regime for brokers of consumer data, and an industry initiative to give web pages special icons that people can use to prevent firms from tracking their activity.

America and Europe will set the global standards. But other countries' privacy rules matter too. China and India will soon have more people online than Europe and America have citizens. Neither Asian country has yet passed formal national legislation, but both are considering it—with every indication that their new laws will outdo even Europe in their severity.

India's draft privacy bill will set up a data-protection authority, call for consent before personal data can be processed, and create a formal "right to privacy". Critics say the bill is too broad and that clauses protecting an individual's "honour and good name" could be used for censorship.

China's draft personal information protection law was proposed in 2003, but has since languished, leading to both regional experimentation and some big ad hoc rulings from ministries. The resulting hotchpotch leaves businesses and consumers confused. But in January 2011 the Ministry of Industry and Information Technology issued draft rules on data protection that restrict the ability of organisations to transfer personal data without specific prior informed consent.

These define personal information broadly, as anything that can identify an individual either on its own, or in combination with other data. They also appear to forbid the export of personal information—even, on one reading, from one division of a company to another. That could hamper multinationals which need to send data across national borders. And it could hit outsourcers trying to deal with their customers. A further danger is that China's regulations are often arbitrarily or selectively enforced. Some information-processing firms are said to have moved their operations to Hong Kong, which has laxer and more predictable rules.

Building a single European data-protection regime is hard enough. Harmonising it smoothly with America will be harder. Reaching deals with Indian bureaucrats and Chinese mandarins set to defend the interests and the data of their countries' rapidly growing online firms may be downright impossible. Welcome to the new world of data geopolitics.

In the United States, the Government Needs to Protect Internet Privacy

The White House

In the following viewpoint, the President Barack Obama administration presents a framework for consumer data privacy to address the privacy issues of new digital technology that includes a consumer privacy bill of rights, codes of conduct for businesses, Federal Trade Commission enforcement of consumers' data privacy rights, and global interoperability. The administration argues in favor of supplemental federal legislation to increase the sectors that are offered legal privacy protection.

As you read, consider the following questions:

1. According to the viewpoint, online retail sales in the United States total how much annually?

2. Why is most personal data used on the Internet not subject to federal legal protection, according to the viewpoint?

3. The administration endorses a consumer privacy bill of rights based on what standards?

The White House, "I. Introduction: Building on the Strength of the US Consumer Data Privacy Framework," *Consumer Data Privacy in a Networked World: A Framework for Protecting Privacy and Promoting Innovation in the Global Digital Economy*, The White House, February 2012, pp. 5–7. Copyright © 2012 The White House. All rights reserved. Republished with permission.

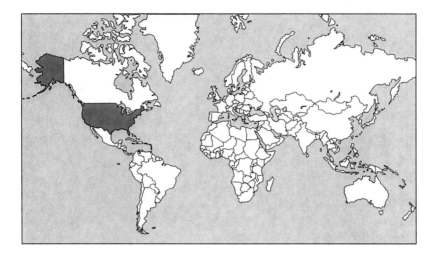

The Internet is integral to economic and social life in the United States and throughout the world. Networked technologies offer individuals nearly limitless ways to express themselves, form social connections, transact business, and organize politically. Networked technologies also spur innovation, enable new business models, and facilitate consumers' and companies' access to information, products, services, and markets across the world.

The Need for Consumer Data Privacy Protections

An abundance of data, inexpensive processing power, and increasingly sophisticated analytical techniques drive innovation in our increasingly networked society. Political organizations and candidates for public office build powerful campaigns on data that individuals share about themselves and their political preferences. Data from social networks allow journalists and individuals to report and follow newsworthy events around the world as they unfold. Data plays a key role in the ability of government to stop identity thieves and protect public safety. Researchers use sets of medical data to identify public health issues and probe the causes of human diseases.

Network operators use data from communications networks to identify events ranging from a severed fiber optic cable to power outages and the acts of malicious intruders. In addition, personal data fuels an advertising marketplace that brings many online services and sources of content to consumers for free.

Strengthening consumer data privacy protections in the United States is an important administration priority. Americans value privacy and expect protection from intrusions by both private and governmental actors. Strong privacy protections also are critical to sustaining the trust that nurtures Internet commerce and fuels innovation. Trust means the companies and technical systems on which we depend meet our expectations for privacy, security, and reliability. In addition, United States leadership in consumer data privacy can help establish more flexible, innovation-enhancing privacy models among our international partners.

Preserving trust in the Internet economy protects and enhances substantial economic activity. Online retail sales in the United States total $145 billion annually. New uses of personal data in location services, protected by appropriate privacy and security safeguards, could create important business opportunities. Moreover, the United States is a world leader in exporting cloud computing, location-based services, and other innovative services. To preserve these economic benefits, consumers must continue to trust networked technologies. Strengthening consumer data privacy protections will help to achieve this goal.

Americans value privacy and expect protection from intrusions by both private and governmental actors.

Preserving trust also is necessary to realize the full social and cultural benefits of networked technologies. When companies use personal data in ways that are inconsistent with the circumstances under which consumers disclosed the data, however, they may undermine trust. For example, individuals who actively share information with their friends, family, colleagues, and the general public through websites and online social networking sites may not be aware of the ways those services, third parties, and their own associates may use information about them. Unauthorized disclosure of sensitive information can violate individual rights, cause injury or discrimination based on sensitive personal attributes, lead to actions and decisions taken in response to misleading or inaccurate information, and contribute to costly and potentially life-disrupting identity theft. Protecting Americans' privacy by preventing identity theft and prosecuting identity thieves is an important focus for the administration.

The United States has both the responsibility and incentive to help establish forward-looking privacy policy models.

A Framework for Protecting Privacy

The existing consumer data privacy framework in the United States is flexible and effectively addresses some consumer data privacy challenges in the digital age. This framework consists of industry best practices, FTC [Federal Trade Commission] enforcement, and a network of chief privacy officers and other privacy professionals who develop privacy practices that adapt to changes in technology and business models and create a growing culture of privacy awareness within companies. Much of the personal data used on the Internet, however, is not subject to comprehensive federal statutory protection, because most federal data privacy statutes apply only to specific sectors, such as health care, education, communications, and financial services or, in the case of online data collection, to children. The administration believes that filling gaps in the existing framework will promote more consistent responses to

The Importance of International Interoperability

The Internet helps U.S. companies expand across borders. As a result, cross-border data flows are a vital component of the domestic and global economies. Differences in national privacy laws create challenges for companies wishing to transfer personal data across national borders. Complying with different privacy laws is burdensome for companies that transfer personal data as part of well-defined, discrete data processing operations because legal standards may vary among jurisdictions, and companies may need to obtain multiple regulatory approvals to conduct even routine operations.

Services that cater to individual users face steeper compliance challenges because they handle data flows that are more complex and varied. Further complicating matters is the proliferation of cloud computing systems. This globally distributed architecture helps deliver cost-effective, innovative new services to consumers, companies, and governments. It also allows consumers and companies to send the personal data they generate and use to recipients all over the world. Consumer data privacy frameworks should not only facilitate these technologies and business models but also adapt rapidly to those that have yet to emerge.

Though governments may take different approaches to meeting these challenges, it is critical to the continued growth of the digital economy that they strive to create interoperability between privacy regimes.

The White House,
Consumer Data Privacy in a Networked World:
A Framework for Protecting Privacy and Promoting Innovation
in the Global Digital Economy, *February 2012, p. 31.*

privacy concerns across the wide range of environments in which individuals have access to networked technologies and in which a broad array of companies collect and use personal data. The administration, however, does not recommend modifying the existing federal statutes that apply to specific sectors unless they set inconsistent standards for related technologies. Instead, the administration supports legislation that would supplement the existing framework and extend baseline protections to the sectors that existing federal statutes do not cover. . . .

As a world leader in Internet innovation, the United States has both the responsibility and incentive to help establish forward-looking privacy policy models that foster innovation and preserve basic privacy rights. The administration's framework for consumer data privacy offers a path toward achieving these goals. It is based on the following key elements:

- A *consumer privacy bill of rights,* setting forth individual rights and corresponding obligations of companies in connection with personal data. These consumer rights are based on U.S.-developed and globally recognized Fair Information Practice Principles (FIPPs), articulated in terms that apply to the dynamic environment of the Internet age;

- *Enforceable codes of conduct,* developed through *multistakeholder processes,* to form the basis for specifying what the consumer privacy bill of rights requires in particular business contexts;

- Federal Trade Commission (FTC) *enforcement* of consumers' data privacy rights through its authority to prohibit unfair or deceptive acts or practices; and

- Increasing *global interoperability* between the U.S. consumer data privacy framework and other countries' frameworks, through mutual recognition, the development of codes of conduct through multi-stakeholder processes, and enforcement cooperation, can reduce barriers to the flow of information.

Countries of the European Union Need Uniform Rules to Protect Data Privacy

European Commission

In the following viewpoint, the European Commission argues that a comprehensive data protection framework is needed for the European Union (EU). The commission claims that a lack of strong and uniform data protection across the member states is creating an environment of consumer distrust, harming online business, and complicating the legal environment. The European Commission is the executive body of the EU responsible for proposing legislation, implementing decisions, upholding treaties, and managing day-to-day business of the EU.

As you read, consider the following questions:

1. According to the European Commission, what is problematic about the protection of personal data in the European Union's 1995 directive?

2. What percentage of Internet users in Europe worry that they are asked for too much personal data online, according to the author?

3. The European Commission claims that a uniform legislative framework on data privacy will remove the fragmentation across how many member states?

European Commission, "Safeguarding Privacy in a Connected World: A European Data Protection Framework for the 21st Century," January 25, 2012. eur-lex.europa.eu.

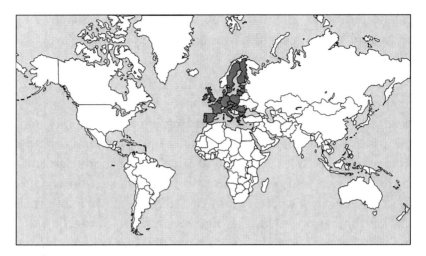

The rapid pace of technological change and globalisation have profoundly transformed the way in which an ever-increasing volume of personal data is collected, accessed, used and transferred. New ways of sharing information through social networks and storing large amounts of data remotely have become part of life for many of Europe's 250 million Internet users. At the same time, personal data has become an asset for many businesses. Collecting, aggregating and analysing the data of potential customers is often an important part of their economic activities.

The Need for Uniform Rules

In this new digital environment, individuals have the right to enjoy effective control over their personal information. Data protection is a fundamental right in Europe, enshrined in article 8 of the Charter of Fundamental Rights of the European Union, as well as in article 16(1) of the Treaty on the Functioning of the European Union (TFEU), and needs to be protected accordingly.

Lack of confidence makes consumers hesitant to buy online and accept new services. Therefore, a high level of data protection is also crucial to enhance trust in online services and to fulfill the potential of the digital economy, thereby encouraging economic growth and the competitiveness of EU [European Union] industries.

Modern, coherent rules across the EU are needed for data to flow freely from one member state to another. Businesses need clear and uniform rules that provide legal certainty and minimise the administrative burden. This is essential if the single market is to function and to stimulate economic growth, create new jobs and foster innovation. A modernisation of the EU's data protection rules, which strengthens their internal market dimension, ensures a high level of data protection for individuals, and promotes legal certainty, clarity and consistency, therefore plays a central role in the European Commission's Stockholm action plan, in the digital agenda for Europe and, more broadly, for the EU's growth strategy Europe 2020.

In this new digital environment, individuals have the right to enjoy effective control over their personal information.

The Reform of Data Protection Rules

The EU's 1995 directive, the central legislative instrument for the protection of personal data in Europe, was a milestone in the history of data protection. Its objectives, to ensure a functioning single market and effective protection of the fundamental rights and freedoms of individuals, remain valid. However, it was adopted 17 years ago when the Internet was in its infancy. In today's new, challenging digital environment, existing rules provide neither the degree of harmonisation required, nor the necessary efficiency to ensure the right to personal data protection. That is why the European Commission is proposing a fundamental reform of the EU's data protection framework.

In addition, the Lisbon Treaty has created, with article 16 of TFEU, a new legal basis for a modernised and comprehensive approach to data protection and the free movement of personal data, also covering police and judicial cooperation in criminal matters. This approach is reflected in the European Commission's communications on the Stockholm programme and the Stockholm action plan, which stress the need for the union to "establish a comprehensive personal data protection scheme covering all areas of EU competence" and "ensure that the fundamental right to data protection is consistently applied".

To prepare the reform of the EU's data protection framework in a transparent manner, the commission has, since 2009, launched public consultations on data protection and engaged in intensive dialogue with stakeholders. On 4 November 2010, the commission published a communication on a comprehensive approach on personal data protection in the European Union which set out the main themes of the reform. Between September and December 2011, the commission was involved in an enhanced dialogue with Europe's national data protection authorities and with the European data protection supervisor to explore options for more consistent application of EU data protection rules across all EU member states.

These discussions made clear that both citizens and businesses wanted the European Commission to reform EU data protection rules in a comprehensive manner. After assessing the impacts of different policy options, the European Commission is now proposing a strong and consistent legislative framework across union policies, enhancing individuals' rights, the single market dimension of data protection and cutting red tape for businesses. The commission proposes that the new framework should consist of:

- A regulation (replacing Directive 95/46/EC) setting out a general EU framework for data protection;

- and a directive (replacing [Council] Framework Decision 2008/977/JHA) setting out rules on the protection of personal data processed for the purposes of prevention, detection, investigation or prosecution of criminal offences and related judicial activities.

This communication sets out the main elements of the reform of the EU framework for data protection.

Control of Personal Data

Under Directive 95/46/EC [also known as the Data Protection Directive]—the EU's main legislative act in the field of data protection today—the ways in which individuals are able to exercise their right to data protection are not sufficiently harmonised across member states. Nor are the powers of the national authorities responsible for data protection harmonised enough to ensure consistent and effective application of the rules. This means that actually exercising such rights is more difficult in some member states than in others, particularly online.

These difficulties are also due to the sheer volume of data collected every day, and the fact that users are often not fully aware that their data is being collected. Although many Europeans consider that disclosure of personal data is increasingly a part of modern life, 72% of Internet users in Europe still worry that they are being asked for too much personal data online. They feel they are not in control of their data. They are not properly informed of what happens to their personal information, to whom it is transmitted and for what purposes. Often, they do not know how to exercise their rights online.

As highlighted in the digital agenda for Europe, concerns about privacy are among the most frequent reasons for people

---

Article 8: Protection of Personal Data

1. Everyone has the right to the protection of personal data concerning him or her.

2. Such data must be processed fairly for specified purposes and on the basis of the consent of the person concerned or some other legitimate basis laid down by law. Everyone has the right of access to data which has been collected concerning him or her, and the right to have it rectified.

3. Compliance with these rules shall be subject to control by an independent authority.

Charter of Fundamental Rights of the European Union, 2000.

---

not buying goods and services online. Given the contribution of the information and communication technology (ICT) sector to overall productivity growth in Europe—20% directly from the ICT sector and 30% from ICT investments—trust in such services is vital to stimulate growth in the EU economy and the competitiveness of European industry.

The aim of the new legislative acts proposed by the commission is to strengthen rights, to give people efficient and operational means to make sure they are fully informed about what happens to their personal data, and to enable them to exercise their rights more effectively.

A Lack of Uniformity

Despite the current directive's objective to ensure an equivalent level of data protection within the EU, there is still considerable divergence in the rules across member states. As a consequence, data controllers may have to deal with 27 different national laws and requirements. The result is a fragmented legal environment which has created legal uncertainty and uneven protection for individuals. This has caused unnecessary costs and administrative burdens for businesses and is a disincentive for enterprises operating in the single market that may want to expand their operations across borders.

Concerns about privacy are among the most frequent reasons for people not buying goods and services online.

The resources and the powers of the national authorities responsible for data protection vary considerably among member states. In some cases, they are unable to perform their enforcement tasks satisfactorily. Cooperation among these authorities at European level—via the existing advisory group (the so-called Article 29 Working Party)—does not always lead to consistent enforcement and also needs to be improved.

National authorities need to be reinforced and their cooperation strengthened to guarantee the consistent enforcement and, ultimately, uniform application of rules across the EU.

A Framework for the EU

A strong, clear and uniform legislative framework at EU level will help to unleash the potential of the digital single market and foster economic growth, innovation and job creation. A regulation will do away with the fragmentation of legal regimes across 27 member states and remove barriers to market entry, a factor of particular importance to micro-, small- and medium-sized enterprises.

The new rules will also give EU companies an advantage in global competition. Under the reformed regulatory framework, they will be able to assure their customers that valuable personal information will be treated with the necessary care and diligence. Trust in a coherent EU regulatory regime will be a key asset for service providers and an incentive for investors looking for optimal conditions when locating services.

The new EU regulation will ensure a robust protection of the fundamental right to data protection throughout the European Union and strengthen the functioning of the single market. At the same time—in view of the fact that, as underlined by the Court of Justice of the EU, the right to the protection of personal data is not an absolute right, but must be considered in relation to its function in society and be balanced with other fundamental rights, in accordance with the principle of proportionality—the regulation will include explicit provisions that ensure the respect of other fundamental rights, such as freedom of expression and information, the right to defence, as well as of professional secrecy (such as for the legal profession), without prejudicing the status of churches under the laws of the member states....

The resources and the powers of the national authorities responsible for data protection vary considerably among member states.

Data Protection in a Globalised World

Individuals' rights must continue to be ensured when personal data is transferred from the EU to third countries, and whenever individuals in member states are targeted and their data is used or analysed by third country service providers. This means that EU data protection standards have to apply regardless of the geographical location of a company or its processing facility.

In today's globalised world, personal data is being transferred across an increasing number of virtual and geographical borders and stored on servers in multiple countries. More companies are offering cloud computing services, which allow customers to access and store data on remote servers. These factors call for an improvement in current mechanisms for transferring data to third countries. This includes adequacy decisions—i.e., decisions certifying 'adequate' data protection standards in third countries—and appropriate safeguards such as standard contractual clauses or binding corporate rules, so as to secure a high level of data protection in international processing operations and facilitate data flows across borders.

The EU data protection reform aims to build a modern, strong, consistent and comprehensive data protection framework for the European Union. Individuals' fundamental right to data protection will be reinforced. Other rights, such as freedom of expression and information, the right of the child, the right to conduct a business, the right to a fair trial and professional secrecy (such as for the legal profession), as well as the status of churches under member states' laws will be respected.

The Benefits of Reform

The reform will first of all benefit individuals by strengthening their data protection rights and their trust in the digital environment. The reform will furthermore simplify the legal environment for businesses and the public sector substantially. This is expected to stimulate the development of the digital economy across the EU's single market and beyond, in line with the objectives of the Europe 2020 strategy and the digital agenda for Europe. Finally, the reform will enhance trust among law enforcement authorities in order to facilitate exchanges of data between them and cooperation in the fight against serious crime, while ensuring a high level of protection for individuals.

The European Commission will work closely with the European Parliament and the council to ensure an agreement on the EU's new data protection framework by the end of 2012. Throughout this adoption process and beyond, especially in the context of the implementation of the new legal instruments, the commission will maintain a close and transparent dialogue with all interested parties involving representatives from the private and public sector. This will include representatives from the police and the judiciary, electronic communications regulators, civil society organisations, data protection authorities and academics, as well as from specialised EU agencies such as Eurojust, Europol, the Fundamental Rights Agency, and the European Network and Information Society Agency.

The EU data protection reform aims to build a modern, strong, consistent and comprehensive data protection framework for the European Union.

In a context of constant development of information technologies and evolving social behaviour, such a dialogue is of the utmost importance to benefit from the input necessary to ensure a high level of data protection of individuals, the growth and competitiveness of EU industries, the operational effectiveness of the public sector (including the police and the judiciary) and a low level of administrative burden.

Different Privacy Protections in Europe and the United States Regulate Social Networking

Anita Ramasastry

In the following viewpoint, Anita Ramasastry argues that privacy concerns regarding Facebook's facial-recognition software have resulted in the disabling of the service in Europe because of the strong data privacy protections. Ramasastry contends that there are legitimate concerns about the collection of biometric data as a default selection, without the explicit opting in by the user. She claims that the United States should take the issue more seriously, as the European Union has done. Ramasastry is the D. Wayne & Anne Gittinger Professor of Law at the University of Washington School of Law in Seattle.

As you read, consider the following questions:

1. According to Ramasastry, in what year did Facebook launch its facial-recognition tag suggestions in the United States?

2. What entity audited Facebook's facial-recognition feature, causing Facebook to stop using the technology in Europe, according to the author?

Anita Ramasastry, "The Right to Be Untagged: As Facebook Disables Facial Recognition for EU Consumers, US Consumers Are Left Wondering What's Next for Them," *Verdict*, September 25, 2012. Copyright © 2012 by Anita Ramasastry. All rights reserved. Reproduced by permission.

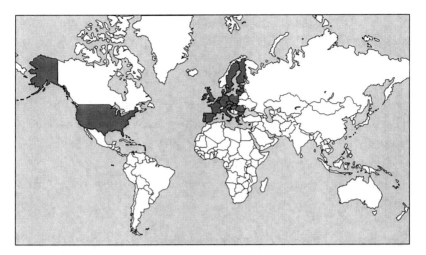

3. According to Ramasastry, the US Federal Trade Commission (FTC) and Facebook reached a settlement in November 2011 regarding what?

Just a few days ago [on September 21, 2012], Facebook announced that it was turning off its facial-recognition tool, which had suggested the identities of registered Facebook users for possible tagging in uploaded photos. Facebook did so in response to an audit by the Irish data protection commissioner, one of 27 national privacy regulators in the EU [European Union]—and the one that happens to be just down the road from Facebook's European headquarters, in Dublin.

A Change in Facebook Policies

At least for now, then, European consumers can rest assured that Facebook will ease up on its practice of scanning photos and suggesting to a person's Facebook friends that a particular photo contains his or her image, and should be tagged accordingly. (Facebook itself does not directly tag people in photos.)

Facebook intends to restore the facial-recognition tool, provided that it can find common ground with regulators about the most appropriate way to obtain user content.

Meanwhile, Facebook has temporarily suspended the auto-tag feature in the U.S. as well. But it had no legal obligation to do so, and thus, the feature may return here soon. [It was re-enabled in the United States on February 1, 2013.]

In this [viewpoint], I will discuss the privacy concerns raised by facial recognition and social networking. I will also discuss why facial recognition is currently off-limits in the EU, based on its privacy law and framework, whereas, in the U.S., we are at the mercy of Facebook's ever-changing privacy terms and business model.

Facebook's Facial-Recognition Feature

Facebook launched its facial-recognition "tag suggestions" feature in the summer of 2010 in the United States. The launch occurred without much fanfare, as often happens with new Facebook features, especially those that may compromise our privacy expectations. In fact, in this case, Facebook introduced the feature by default, forcing users who disliked the concept to opt out and to do so in a cumbersome way, by navigating Facebook's constantly changing privacy settings to opt out of suggested tags. It is even harder to request that stored tagged photos be deleted, via a hard-to-find link.

As noted above, the service is opt out (not opt in) in Facebook's privacy settings—with the default being that you are set up to be tagged unless you object. And that aspect of the facial-recognition feature, and of Facebook's approach to privacy generally, bothers privacy advocates.

Facebook added facial recognition to its site after buying Israeli startup Face.com for a reported $100 million. The feature automatically checks to see if users' friends appear in images that they upload, and suggests friends to tag, ensuring that identifiable images will be shared more widely and appear on the home pages of the tagged user. Thus, even if you have never posted a photo of yourself, you may find your page populated with photos taken by others, where you are "tagged."

Facebook's facial-recognition technology works by generating a biometric signature for users who are tagged in photos on Facebook using data from "photo comparisons." This biometric "signature," based on scanning of a user's facial image, is available to Facebook, but not to the user.

The service is opt out (not opt in) in Facebook's privacy settings—with the default being that you are set up to be tagged unless you object.

Facebook's Biometric-Data Collection

Facebook routinely encourages users to "tag"—that is, to provide actual identifying names for themselves, their friends and acquaintances, and other people they may recognize on the site. Facebook then associates the tags with a user's account, compares what the tagged photos have in common, and stores a summary of the comparison. Facebook notes that it automatically compares uploaded photos "to the summary information we've stored about what your tagged photos have in common."

When Facebook introduced its auto-tagging, it gave no special notice to users, and failed to obtain their consent prior to collecting and storing biometric data and facial comparisons. Put more simply, Facebook was creating a large archive of our images—linking those images to our name, our identity, and other data about us—without providing us with any other notice about this facial-recognition technology. Facebook admitted in a later statement, "[W]e should have been clearer during the roll-out process when this became available to [users]."

Moreover, there is no option within a user's Facebook privacy preferences to delete or prevent Facebook's biometric-data collection. Instead, if a user wants to delete this "summary" data associated with his account that can be used to couple his name to photos of him, the user must contact Facebook through a difficult-to-find link.

Photo-tagging is important for Facebook, as it allows the social network to better ascertain the persons with whom its users interact in the real world, and to try and make money off of these associations in the future. It also allows Facebook, via tagging, to figure out where we travel, what we do, and whom we like.

Three Concerns About Facebook's Software

Some readers may wonder, why would anyone care about their image being identified, with the help of fellow users, through Facebook's software? There are a few good reasons for concern.

First, it seems creepy to know that a company is keeping an archive of photos of us without our affirmative consent—thus creating a digital photo album displaying who we are, where we have been, and with whom we associate.

Second, the tagging feature relies on getting third parties to identify other Facebook users, which is also a bit unsettling.

And third—and arguably worst of all—a database is being created, without the user's consent, that could someday be accessed for intelligence or law enforcement purposes. Governments in democracies and repressive regimes alike would love to have access to such a trove of images—to help them identify people ranging from protesters at a demonstration, to crime suspects.

European Union Privacy Law

As questions from users, privacy advocates, and regulators have mounted with respect to Facebook and its method of user-enabled facial recognition, Facebook quietly and temporarily pulled the plug on "tag suggestions" for all Facebook users this past summer.

Facebook did not introduce facial-recognition features in Europe until June 2011. Yet, within the year, Irish data protection (i.e., privacy) commissioners started to raise concerns about the practice.

A database is being created, without the user's consent, that could someday be accessed for intelligence or law enforcement purposes.

Moreover, EU privacy regulators—including the data protecting commissions in Norway, Germany, and Ireland—have voiced concerns about Facebook's facial recognition, worrying that the feature violates EU privacy laws.

The EU has a comprehensive privacy law, the Data Protection Directive [officially known as Directive 95/46/EC], which is implemented through national privacy legislation in member countries. Those laws require that companies (1) obtain consent before they collect a user's personal data, including images, and (2) notify the user when they are going to collect or use data in a new manner. Thus, when Facebook unveiled the recognition/tagging feature, European regulators believed that Facebook had not properly gotten consent by asking users to "opt in" and thus permit the use of their data.

Moreover, in the EU, citizens have a right to access information that a company collects about them, and to have that information deleted if they so choose. It was unclear whether Facebook was still compiling tagged photos of users—even if it was no longer posting those tagged photos online—without user consent. In other words, there was a fear that Facebook was amassing a database of tagged user images, and keeping that database in storage, even if it was respecting our wishes not to have our photos tagged by other users online.

Facebook User Complaints

Based on Facebook user complaints, the Irish data protection commissioner (DPC) audited Facebook's facial-recognition feature. In late September, it announced the audit's results, revealing that Facebook intends to delete its facial-recognition data and stop using the technology in Europe next month, as it works to comply with the privacy watchdog in addressing user complaints.

The EU has a comprehensive privacy law, the Data Protection Directive, which is implemented through national privacy legislation in member countries.

Last October, for example, Australian law student Max Schrems lodged a reported 22 complaints with the Irish privacy watchdog after requesting a copy of his data from Facebook. Schrems discovered that Facebook had kept all of his deleted data.

Since then, Facebook has stopped using facial-recognition technology for new users in Europe. For existing users, Facebook will deactivate its service throughout Europe on October 15.

The audit—conducted to ascertain whether the company had adjusted its practices to conform with Irish and EU data protection laws—found that Facebook has now implemented many of the privacy improvements that were suggested in a previous government report. It cites improved transparency regarding how data is handled, better user control over Facebook settings, greater clarity about data retention and deletion capabilities, and enhanced user data-access rights.

"I am particularly encouraged in relation to the approach [Facebook] has decided to adopt on the tag suggest/facial-recognition feature by in fact agreeing to go beyond our initial recommendations, in light of developments since then, in order to achieve best practice," DPC head Billy Hawkes said. He added that Facebook's actions demonstrated a clear commitment to good data protection practice.

Unresolved Issues

However, while the Irish DPC applauded Facebook's ceasing its facial-recognition program, several other issues remain unresolved. The regulator has raised questions about whether Facebook is actually deleting photos that are marked for removal within 40 days, as required under Irish data protection laws.

The Irish DPC also seeks further clarification about the way Facebook handles inactive and deactivated accounts. The Irish privacy watchdog has given Facebook another four weeks to address this issue.

Richard Allan, Facebook's director of policy for Europe, the Middle East, and Africa, says the decision to remove the facial-recognition tool was made in response to new guidance issued by the EU. Allan said, "Our intention is to reinstate the tag-suggest feature, but consistent with new guidelines. The service will need a different form of notice and consent."

That's a major admission for Facebook, acknowledging that the site will improve its notice and consent practices with respect to EU consumers.

If Facebook does reintroduce its facial-recognition mechanism, users will have to opt in, not opt out. Also at issue is whether Facebook will maintain images of people who do not consent to the collection of those images. Thus, in the EU, users may find that they have had their images deleted, and that Facebook will not initiate scanning and suggested tags without their affirmative permission.

A Complaint in the United States

While EU regulators have explicit authority to stop Facebook's data collection unless it complies with EU law, the situation in the U.S. is different. Currently, in the U.S., Facebook is able to use facial recognition—and to require users to opt out, rather than opting in. Moreover, Facebook can do so without much fear of legal repercussions, because here in the U.S., there is no federal privacy law that regulates how Facebook can collect our biometric data.

In 2010, when Facebook launched its service, the Electronic Privacy Information Center (EPIC), a leading U.S. privacy NGO [nongovernmental organization], filed a complaint with the U.S. Federal Trade Commission (FTC), complaining about the way that facial recognition was deployed, three days after Facebook launched "tag suggestions."

The complaint alleged that: (1) Facebook is involved in "unfair and deceptive acts and practices" due to its continued use of the automatic-tagging feature; (2) Facebook's implementation of the facial-recognition technology is an invasion of privacy, which not only causes harm to consumers, but is done without their consent; and (3) Facebook's collection of biometric data from children is contrary to the Children's Online Privacy Protection Act of 1988 (COPPA).

Here in the U.S., there is no federal privacy law that regulates how Facebook can collect our biometric data.

Additionally, the EPIC complaint requests that the FTC require Facebook to: (1) immediately suspend Facebook-initiated tagging or identification of users based on Facebook's database of facial images; (2) not misrepresent how it "maintains and protects the security, privacy, confidentiality, and integrity of any consumer information"; and (3) provide additional disclosures to users prior to new or additional sharing of information with third parties.

Opting In vs. Opting Out

The EPIC complaint focuses on Facebook's business practices because the FTC is equipped to pursue such violations under section 5(a) of the FTC Act [Federal Trade Commission Act], which focuses on preventing unfair or deceptive trade practices. The FTC Act, however, is not a comprehensive privacy statute, and does not require companies to obtain consent before collecting consumer data. To the contrary, unlike the EU, the U.S. typically allows a company's terms of service (ToS), a private contract, to set the privacy commitments that a company makes to its customers. That is why, in the U.S., Facebook will introduce a new feature (such as Timeline or auto-tagging) and require users to opt out, rather than opt in. This approach, of course, takes advantage of inertia—as many users may not be aware of a change in privacy practices, or may not take the time to opt out—especially if it must be done by links that are hard to find, and/or instructions that are difficult to understand.

With respect to Facebook and photo-tagging, EPIC noted in its complaint that:

"Facebook users are only given the option to turn off the automatic-tagging feature and have their biometric data deleted only after the feature is installed. To turn off this feature, a user must navigate through his or her privacy settings to 'opt out' of the tag suggestion service. In addition to opting out, a user has to send a message to Facebook and specifically request that Facebook delete the data that it has collected. This multi-layered process is confusing and there is no instruction page or notification alerting users that opting out is an option."

The bottom line: EPIC asked the FTC to prohibit Facebook from creating facial-recognition profiles without getting users' express consent.

The EPIC complaint also explains how Facebook has failed to establish that application developers, the government, and other third parties will not be able to access Facebook's "photo comparison data." It also addresses the ways in which Facebook's collection of biometric data for facial recognition violates user expectations and its own ToS.

The Future of Facebook Policies

It's not surprising, however, that EPIC's complaint is currently still pending with the FTC. The FTC can act, if it believes a complaint has merit, but it is not obliged to do so. And the FTC recently dealt with Facebook. In November 2011, the two reached a settlement relating to other privacy problems the company had, in terms of its sharing data with third parties.

As part of the FTC settlement, Facebook must implement practices that are appropriate to the sensitivity of the "covered information" in question, which is very broadly defined in the order, and would include biometric data.

The most hopeful development here is that when Facebook plans to override our privacy preferences in the future, it is meant to obtain our affirmative consent. But it appears that facial recognition and auto-tagging were already grandfathered in. Thus, there may be no need for Facebook to go back and get our permission with respect to these features—meaning that American users may still be stuck with auto-tagging, unless we expressly opt out.

Finally, based on what Facebook did with Timeline—forcing us to switch to the new profile whether we wanted to or not, it appears that the concept of affirmative consent to Facebook changes may be more mythical than we might once have hoped.

Lawmakers' Concern About Privacy

In addition to scrutiny from European regulators, Facebook has faced criticism from U.S. lawmakers over its use of facial-recognition technology. At a Senate hearing last July, Senator Al Franken (D. Minn.), described Facebook as the "world's largest privately held database of face prints—without the explicit consent of its users."

Last Friday, after Facebook's EU announcement, Senator Franken said in an email statement that he hoped that Facebook would offer a way for American users to opt in to its photographic database.

"I believe that we have a fundamental right to privacy, and that means people should have the ability to choose whether or not they'll be enrolled in a commercial facial-recognition database," he said. "I encourage Facebook to provide the same privacy protections to its American users as it does its foreign ones."

The idea that a private company is amassing a large database of photos of us is creepy.

A Tale of Two Jurisdictions

To recap, EU citizens have regulators watching out for them, and a specific right to opt in to new uses of data by Facebook. Meanwhile, in the U.S., the FTC settlement—at least in theory—means that Facebook should check with us before launching new tools and applications that use our data and images in surprising new ways.

But the FTC settlement is still ambiguous. It does not create an explicit statutory mandate for Facebook to treat us and our data in a certain way. In contrast, the current White House proposal (which now also appears in pending federal legislation) would give us an explicit statutory bill of rights in this area.

Should we be concerned? As I noted above, the idea that a private company is amassing a large database of photos of us is creepy. Moreover, the database may well be seen by Facebook as a large asset, in which it has property rights that it can then monetize.

Other businesses also see commercial potential here. For example, Redpepper, an Atlanta-based company, is developing an application to allow Facebook users to be identified by cameras installed in stores and restaurants. Redpepper has reported in a blog post that users would have to authorize the application to pull their most recently tagged photographs. After you give consent, Redpepper says, "custom-developed cameras then simply use this existing data to identify you in the real world," including by offering you special discounts and deals.

Europe's Ongoing Battles with Facebook

Meanwhile, it's useful to remember that we're still in the early days when it comes to Facebook's use of photo-tagging in the EU, and the regulation that may well follow. In addition to Ireland's probe, Germany recently called the practice of photo-tagging illegal, and demanded that Facebook disable its facial-recognition service and destroy its German database of user images derived from facial recognition.

Facebook said at the time that it didn't have to do so, because the data collection is legal in Ireland, where the company has its European headquarters. But Irish privacy authorities were conducting an inquiry of their own, and they forced Facebook to partially do what Germany had demanded.

In Germany, meanwhile, the Hamburg commissioner for data protection and freedom of information has issued an administrative order against Facebook over its facial-recognition technology, in the midst of the country's own ongoing battle with Facebook. This measure appears to have been taken more or less independently of whatever was happening in Dublin. According to the Hamburg regulator, if Facebook cannot sort it out, "the existing database has to be deleted." That rule would apply only to Hamburg, although, the commissioner notes, "Other German authorities have already announced similar administration procedures."

Although Ireland's decision has wider EU ramifications because Facebook's international headquarters are in that country, Hamburg maintains that Facebook still needs to comply with local regulations in Germany. And so EU privacy regulators continue on with their push to keep Facebook accountable to EU consumers.

Internet Laws a Sledgehammer Approach to Privacy

Chris Berg

In the following viewpoint, Chris Berg warns that the danger of "bad laws" regarding the Internet is an issue regardless of where one lives. Berg claims that a recent European Union proposal threatens to stifle online speech. He urges Australians to be concerned about Europe's legislation since it will affect them and its ramifications are likely to spread. Berg is a research fellow with the Institute of Public Affairs and editor of the IPA Review. *He is the author of* The Growth of Australia's Regulatory State: Ideology, Accountability and the Mega-Regulators.

As you read, consider the following questions:

1. Berg argues that what US law is an example of a bad law that stifles online liberties?

2. Berg contends that what European Union (EU) laws pose a threat to freedom of speech?

3. According to the author, the EU's proposed privacy laws not only run the risk of violating free speech, they also pose what risk?

Chris Berg, "Internet Laws a Sledgehammer Approach to Privacy," *Sydney Morning Herald* (Australia), February 12, 2012. Copyright © 2012 by Sydney Morning Herald. All rights reserved. Republished with permission.

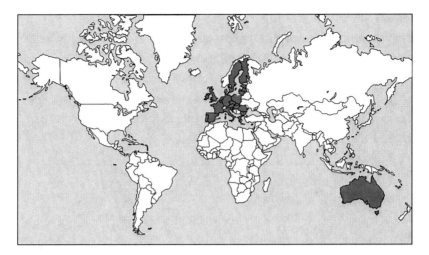

The protest against the American Stop Online Piracy Act recently, where Wikipedia and 7000 other websites went dark for 24 hours, made two things plain.

First, online activism can be effective. Before the protest, 31 members of Congress opposed the act. After the protest, that number swelled to 122. The bill died overnight.

More importantly, the protest emphasised that the Internet is not the Wild West. Domestic laws and international treaties pervade everything we do online. And bad laws can cause profound damage.

The Stop Online Piracy Act (SOPA) is an example of legislative over-reach. SOPA would have given the US government broad powers to shut down access to foreign sites that were suspected of hosting material that breached copyright. This would have given governments the power to interfere with the internal workings of the Internet. Such a power would have been an unconscionable threat to free speech.

Yet SOPA is not alone. The Internet is surprisingly vulnerable to laws that, with good intentions or bad, have the potential to stifle online liberties. Take for instance, the European Union's proposed "right to be forgotten". Changes to data protection laws now being considered by the European Parliament would give Internet users the power to force websites to delete information about them.

There would be privacy benefits from this law. No question it would be lovely if we could make websites remove embarrassing photos or uncomfortable facts years after we uploaded them.

Censorship to protect privacy is just as dangerous as censorship to prevent piracy.

And yes, we need to keep pressure on social networks to protect our privacy. Too many companies are reckless with user data. Yet the EU's plan goes way too far. A legislated "right to be forgotten" would be, like SOPA, a threat to freedom of speech. These new rules would, according to the American legal scholar Jane Yakowitz, "give EU residents an unprecedented inalienable right to control and delete facts that were once voluntarily communicated".

In the age of social media we all happily put information about ourselves in the public domain. A right to be forgotten is actually an obligation for others to forget things they've been told.

Apart from being unworkable (erasing stuff from the Internet is a lot more complicated than politicians seem to believe), this new obligation would envelop the Internet in a legal quagmire.

The law would turn every Internet user into a potential censor, with a veto over everything they've ever revealed about themselves. Every time media organisations referred to freely obtained information, they would have to be sure they could prove they did so for a "legitimate" news purpose. This would create enormous difficulties for journalism. Censorship to protect privacy is just as dangerous as censorship to prevent piracy.

But unlike SOPA, there has been no outcry about these new rules. No blackout of popular websites, no mass petitions.

SOPA was driven by American politicians in the thrall of an unpopular copyright lobby. The European data protection rules are being driven by social democrats claiming to protect people's privacy. And, in 2012, privacy is a value that many people claim to rate above all others.

By contrast, free speech seems daggy and unpopular. Even our self-styled civil liberties groups have downgraded their support for freedom of speech. Now other rights—privacy is one, the right not to be offended is another—are seen as more important. So these new laws could slip through with disastrous consequences.

Should Australians care what the European Parliament does? Absolutely. The big Internet firms are global. If a legislature in one country or continent changes the rules of the game, those firms have to comply. The easiest way to comply is by making global policy changes, not regional ones.

And regulations introduced overseas have a habit of eventually being introduced in Australia. Already our privacy activists are talking up the EU scheme.

Whatever the EU decides about a right to be forgotten, it will have significant effects on the online services we use in Victoria.

Free speech isn't the only problem with the EU's proposed privacy laws. As Jane Yakowitz points out, people trade information with corporations all the time—for discounts or access to free services. No one compels us to share stuff on the Internet. We share because we think we'll get something out of it. The new right to be forgotten would make such trades virtually impossible. It could cripple the information economy overnight.

Governments have always struggled to legislate for the online world. Not only do politicians have little understanding of the technological issues, but the Internet doesn't take very well to regulation: According to one old tech saying, "the net interprets censorship as damage, and routes around it". So legislators over-compensate.

The Internet is complex, borderless and dynamic. Laws are inflexible and heavy-handed. Too many attempts to protect privacy or combat copyright infringement take a brickbat to freedom of expression and Internet liberties.

Periodical and Internet Sources Bibliography

The following articles have been selected to supplement the diverse views presented in this chapter.

American Civil Liberties Union — "Understanding the Risk," March 16, 2011. www.aclu.org.

Peter Bright — "Europe Proposes a 'Right to Be Forgotten,'" Ars Technica, January 25, 2012. http://arstechnica.com.

John Hendel — "Why Journalists Shouldn't Fear Europe's 'Right to Be Forgotten,'" *Atlantic*, January 25, 2012.

Marcia Hofmann, Rainey Reitman, and Cindy Cohn — "When the Government Comes Knocking, Who Has Your Back?," Electronic Frontier Foundation, May 31, 2012. www.eff.org.

Cecilia Kang — "Parting with Privacy with a Quick Click," *Washington Post*, May 8, 2011.

Alex Masters — "Facebook 'Privacy Notice' Hoax: We Know Too Little About Online Privacy," *Independent* (UK), October 3, 2012.

Tessa Mayes — "We Have No Right to Be Forgotten Online," *Guardian* (UK), March 18, 2011.

Jeffrey Rosen — "The Right to Be Forgotten," *Stanford Law Review*, February 13, 2012.

David Shamah — "Security Expert: Faster, Smarter Cyber Thieves Turning Internet into Data Free-for-All," *Times of Israel*, June 7, 2012.

Jason Walsh — "Facebook on Collision Course with New EU Privacy Laws," *Christian Science Monitor*, February 3, 2012.

 GLOBALVIEWPOINTS

 CHAPTER 3

Privacy and Sexuality and Reproduction

In the United Kingdom, Public Abortion Statistics Threaten Women's Privacy

Kate Smurthwaite

In the following viewpoint, Kate Smurthwaite argues that allowing statistics on late-term abortions to be released to the public threatens to expose the identity of women who have had abortions later than twenty-four weeks gestation. Smurthwaite contends that women who have late-term abortions do so for a range of fetal conditions and that these women should not have to justify their case to the media. Smurthwaite is vice chair of the United Kingdom organization Abortion Rights as well as an active member of London Feminist Network, a women-only feminist networking and campaigning organization.

As you read, consider the following questions:

1. According to the author, data on termination of pregnancies after twenty-four weeks will be aggregated for conditions affecting how many cases?

2. Smurthwaite claims that the number of late-term abortions each year is fairly consistent, averaging approximately how many?

Kate Smurthwaite, "An Abortion Ruling That Puts the Privacy of Women at Risk," *Guardian* (UK), April 22, 2011. Copyright © 2011 by Guardian News & Media Ltd. All rights reserved. Reproduced by permission.

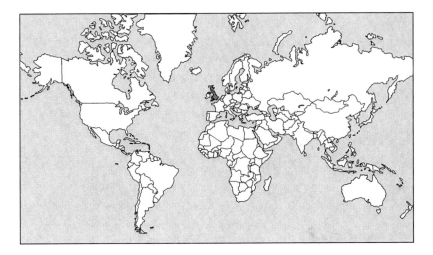

3. What negative effect does the author claim has resulted from ethics committees created to approve late-term abortions?

Following a recent ruling at the information tribunal that will allow late abortion figures to be released, vulnerable bereaved parents and their clinicians are being put at risk of being doorstepped by tabloid journalists, or forced into lengthy and expensive legal battles.

A Challenge to Information Privacy

The Department of Health [DH] had argued that while data on the medical grounds for termination of pregnancies after 24 weeks should be provided, it was in the interest of patient and practitioner confidentiality to aggregate conditions affecting 10 or less cases. More detailed breakdowns would be made available, aggregated over five or 10 years.

Importantly, the challenge to the DH's stance does not come from a neutral academic research body in need of clearer data for medical research. It comes from the ProLife Alliance, an overtly anti-choice campaign group with a clear and stated agenda to completely end the provision of abortion services in the UK [United Kingdom]. Combined with information already in the public domain, the details released could help identify women having late-term abortions and make them vulnerable to harassment by anti-abortion campaigners and tabloid journalists. This is a travesty of justice.

Harriet S (not her real name), a woman in her 30s, told me: "You don't get to six or seven months of pregnancy with a child you're feeling lacking and then decide you're going to terminate for trivial reasons. There are extremely serious conditions, many of which are terminal. In my case, it wasn't a question of if the baby survived but of when it died." It's obvious how much her late-term abortion has affected her when she adds, "We had painted the nursery."

I've changed Harriet's name, of course, to allow her to tell her story without risk of being identified. But the ruling means that she, others like her and the clinicians who support these women could have their identities exposed.

Combined with information already in the public domain, the details released could help identify women having late-term abortions.

A Wide Variety of Fetal Abnormalities

In 2009, there were 136 abortions in the UK among women who had passed 24 weeks of pregnancy. Numbers are fairly consistent—around the 130 mark each year. The range of conditions involved is very wide, predominantly involving a variety of brain and cardiac abnormalities; most common foetal abnormalities, such as Down's syndrome, are typically revealed earlier in pregnancy at the 12- or 20-week scan. As such, many conditions will be listed with only one or two cases a year, effectively providing one individual woman's medical record.

Gestation Weeks of Legal Abortions in England and Wales, 2011

Gestation Weeks	Total Number of Abortions
3–8	130,385
9–12	42,791
13–19	14,026
20–23[1]	2,583
Over 24 weeks[1]	146
Total	**189,931**

[1] 24 weeks and 0 days gestation is included in 23 weeks because the legislation distinguishes between abortions up to 24 weeks and over 24 weeks.

TAKEN FROM: Department of Health, "Abortion Statistics, England and Wales: 2011," May 2012. www.wp.dh.gov.uk.

Single tick-box categories fail to provide a real understanding of cases anyway. Many conditions may interact with other medical problems or known genetic issues within a family. Others exist on a spectrum, or can be symptoms of more serious underlying conditions.

When similar information was leaked in 2001, a court case was brought by Church of England vicar Joanna Jepson against doctors accused of performing a late termination on grounds of a cleft lip and palate. No mention was made of the fact that the condition exists across a wide range of severity and can indicate an underlying genetic problem. The details of the case were never made public but it was immediately thrown out of court on the grounds of "no case to answer".

In the wake of the Jepson case, some clinics felt compelled to establish ethics committees, leaving parents reeling from bad news waiting up to two weeks for permission to proceed with a termination. Ultimately, we are creating a situation where clinicians feel they have to justify their decisions on a case-by-case basis to the national media. There is also concern that reduced confidentiality will make women more reluctant to participate in medical research that could lead to earlier diagnosis and better preventative and therapeutic treatment options for serious medical conditions.

The Impact on Women

To date, the ProLife Alliance's tactics have included sending plastic models of foetuses to MPs [members of Parliament], operating "help lines" intended to mislead women about the risks of abortion and holding vigils outside family planning centres. It seems clear that any opportunity to launch a legal challenge on any aspect of abortion or to kick up a media storm will be seized upon.

Ultimately, we are creating a situation where clinicians feel they have to justify their decisions on a case-by-case basis to the national media.

Jane Fisher is the director of Antenatal Results and Choices (ARC), the UK's only non-directive organisation supporting women who are given diagnoses of foetal abnormality. She tells me that:

"ARC has regular contact with women who are given the devastating news late in pregnancy that their baby has a potentially lethal or severely disabling condition. Reeling from the shock of this news they face the life-changing decision about whether to continue or end their wanted pregnancy. It is a very traumatic time and they need to be enabled to make the decision that's right for them with an absolute guarantee of privacy and confidentiality. These are also challenging and distressing situations for clinicians. All parties involved in such harrowing circumstances need our trust, support and compassion, rather than suspicion or judgement."

This ruling will do nothing to advance the well-being of those involved in decisions around late termination. All it will do is leave them paranoid that whatever normality they've managed to find after the loss of a child could suddenly be ripped away.

In Europe, Genetic Diagnosis Is Protected by the Right to Privacy

Antonia Latsch

In the following viewpoint, Antonia Latsch contends the European Court of Human Rights has established that the right to privacy forbids European countries from prohibiting embryo screening for disease through preimplantation diagnosis and genetic testing while authorizing abortion when the same disease is detected in a fetus. She notes that the court stopped short of claiming there is a right to the biotechnologies but found that an Italian law prohibiting such screening for disease unduly restricted the privacy rights of the prospective parents. Latsch is a foreign legal specialist at Public International Law and Policy Group, Dean's Fellow at Academy on Human Rights and Humanitarian Law, and a columnist for the Human Rights Brief.

As you read, consider the following questions:

1. According to Latsch, article 8 of the European Convention on Human Rights offers protection of what?
2. What did the European Court of Human Rights rule in its decision in *S.H. and Others v. Austria*, according to the author?

Antonia Latsch, "Italy's Embryo Screening Ban Breached Couple's Right to Privacy," *Human Rights Brief*, December 29, 2012. Copyright © 2012 by Human Rights Brief. All rights reserved. Republished with permission.

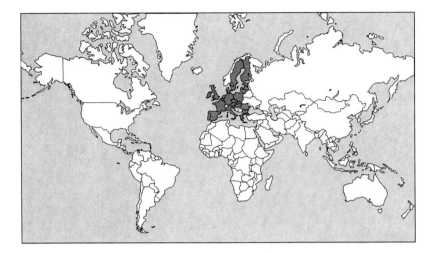

3. How many European countries have yet to establish laws regulating in vitro fertilization, according to Latsch?

The European Court of Human Rights (ECtHR) delivered its judgment in the bioethics case of *Costa and Pavan v. Italy*, holding the state responsible for violating article 8 of the European Convention on Human Rights (ECHR) by prohibiting prenatal diagnosis of genetic diseases. The ECtHR found in its August 10, 2012, decision that the Italian law on human-assisted reproduction violated the right to privacy by creating inconsistent and disproportionate interference in the applicants' lives by denying them access to embryo screening but authorising medically assisted termination of pregnancy when the fetus showed symptoms of the same disease.

The Right to Privacy

With the help of in vitro fertilization, in which the egg is fertilized outside the woman's body, and genetic screening, the applicants, both carriers of cystic fibrosis, wanted to avoid transmitting the disease to their offspring. Because the Italian law prohibits preimplantation diagnosis, their only option was to conceive and medically terminate it if the fetus tested positive for the disease. The couple argued that not being able to access genetic screening to select an embryo unaffected by the disease was a violation of articles 8 and 14 of the ECHR.

Article 8 of the ECHR offers general protection of a person's private and family life, home, and correspondence against arbitrary interference by the state. Section 2 of article 8 specifies that public authority cannot interfere with this right unless it "is in accordance with the law and is necessary . . . for the protection of health or morals, or for the protection of the rights and freedoms of others." The Italian government did not dispute that the law fell within the scope of article 8; however, it argued that the ban legitimately intervened to protect the health of mother and child, the doctor's conscience, and the public interest to prevent eugenic selection.

The court found the law interfered with the couple's right to respect for their private and family life.

The Court's Ruling

In its ruling against Italy, the court highlighted "the incoherence of the Italian legislative system that only bans the implantation of healthy embryos while allowing the abortion of fetuses with genetic conditions." By preventing them from proceeding in this manner, the court found the law interfered with the couple's right to respect for their private and family life. The court accordingly considered that the interference with the applicants' right to respect for their private and family life was disproportionate and breached article 8 of the ECHR. The ruling is consistent with a previous decision by the court in *S.H. [and Others] v. Austria* upholding a law prohibiting in vitro fertilization, on the grounds that there was no European consensus to consider it a protected human right, but the decision allowed for an exception, as was found in the *Costa and Pavan* case, where the public interests do not outweigh the private ones. Also like in the *S.H.* case, the court in *Costa and Pavan* declined to enter into bioethical issues and rule that prohibition of access to preimplantation genetic diagnosis is incompatible with the ECHR and instead restated the importance of proportionality, here related to the prohibition of preimplantation genetic diagnosis with regard to the authorization of therapeutic abortion. The court also declined to recognize a violation of article 14, the prohibition on discrimination, because the law applied to all and would not inform of the results of a test in cases where man tested positive for a sexually transmitted disease.

The court held the notion of "private life" to be a broad concept inclusive of the right to respect for one's decision to have or not to have a child.

The court found in 2007 that the right of a couple to make use of in vitro fertilization to conceive a child can be protected by article 8 as an expression of private and family life. The case concerned two Austrian couples who wanted to conceive a child through in vitro fertilization but were denied access by Austrian law. *Costa and Pavan v. Italy* broadened the scope of private and family life provided protection under article 8 by including the desire to have a child born healthy and without genetically transmissible diseases. By identifying the parents' *wish* with their right to privacy, the court projected the concept of article 8 as a right of individual will in social order. Thus, the *desire* to have a child free from disease constitutes an aspect of the right to privacy granted by article 8. The court held the notion of "private life" to be a broad concept inclusive of the right to respect for one's decision to have or not to have a child. Furthermore, the court observed that the terms "child" and "embryo" must not be confused, opposing the government's argument that the ban legitimately intervened to protect the health of the child. Accordingly, to avoid any deviation in the field of eugenics and to protect the freedom of conscience of medical personnel, the term "child" would not apply.

The majority of European countries allow some form of in vitro fertilization to avoid the inheritance of genetic diseases. Twelve European countries have yet to establish laws regulating in vitro fertilization, although some, such as Poland, are currently considering legislation. The court's decision in this case sets binding precedent for all Council of Europe members, obligating Poland to consider the court's decision when developing its policy. Given the developments in the field of artificial procreation, access to preimplantation genetic screening gives rise to many ethical questions, and given the human rights implications, the legislative decisions will fall under the supervision of the ECtHR—which has thus far shown a focus on considerations of the rights of individuals but not to make broader, bioethical decisions. The court's ruling comes at a time when prenatal diagnosis and in vitro fertilization are just two of many possibilities for altering human reproduction. Although the court has taken a stand on the relevance of reproductive medicine to the protection of private and family life, it remains unclear how in vitro fertilization can or should be protected by the European human rights system.

Nigeria's Proposed Same-Sex Marriage Ban Violates Rights, Including the Right to Privacy

Damian Ugwu

In the following viewpoint, Damian Ugwu argues that a proposed law to prohibit same-sex marriage that creates offenses and penalties for participation in or witnessing of such marriages is a violation of rights guaranteed by the Nigerian Constitution and international human rights treaties. Ugwu claims the bill, if enacted, threatens to incite discrimination and other human rights violations. Ugwu is the regional program coordinator for Africa at the International Gay and Lesbian Human Rights Commission.

As you read, consider the following questions:

1. According to Ugwu, section 5 of Nigeria's proposed law provides for how many years of imprisonment for engaging in same-sex marriage?

2. Ugwu claims that the bill in question violates what two international human rights treaties to which Nigeria is party?

3. According to the author, article 7 of the Universal Declaration of Human Rights prohibits what?

Damian Ugwu, "Nigerian Same-Sex Marriage Ban Infringes Individual Rights," *Jurist*, December 16, 2011. Copyright © 2011 by the Jurist. All rights reserved. Republished with permission.

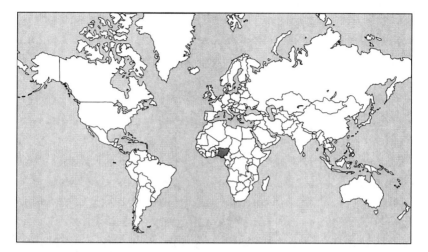

On November 29, 2011, the Nigerian Senate unanimously passed a bill prohibiting same-sex marriage and further criminalizing homosexuality. The legislation, "A Bill for an Act to Prohibit Marriage or Civil Union Entered into Between Persons of Same Sex, Solemnization of Same and for Other Matters Related Therewith," was first introduced by Senator Domingo Banda and 24 others and went through a public hearing organized by the Senate Committee on Judiciary, Health and Human Rights. It is expected that the bill will go through the House of Representatives [passed November 2012] and will be sent to the president for final accent and passage into law. Against the background of worldwide indignation from groups, governments and the public debate ignited by the bill, this [viewpoint] looks at the bill and tries to explain its implications for individual liberties and human rights in Nigeria.

Nigeria's Same-Sex Marriage Bill

The same-sex marriage bill is divided into 8 sections:

Section 1 prohibits marriage between same-sex persons in Nigeria. Section 1(3) voids any marriage between persons of the same sex entered into in other countries and deprives such couples the recognition or entitlement to the benefits of a valid marriage. It also makes any contractual or other rights accruing as a result of any same-sex marriage unenforceable in any court in Nigeria.

Section 2 prohibits the celebration of same-sex marriage at religious centers and the issuance of marriage licenses to parties of the same sex.

Section 4 prohibits the registration of gay clubs and societies in all institutions and publicity of same-sex sexual relationships. The section further prohibits publicity, procession and public show of a same-sex amorous relationship.

Section 5 creates the offenses and penalties for holding same-sex marriages, or for performing, witnessing or aiding or abetting the ceremony of same-sex marriages. Engaging in same-sex marriage is punishable by 14 years' imprisonment, while the crime of participating in gay organizations, public show of amorous same-sex relationship, witnessing and abetting the solemnization of same-sex marriage, registering or supporting the registration and operation of gay clubs, societies and organizations in Nigeria attracts a penalty of 10 years' imprisonment.

Section 6 confers the jurisdiction to entertain all matters, cases and proceedings arising from same-sex marriages or relationships on the high court in the states and the Federal Capital Territory.

Justification for the Bill

While introducing the bill at the floor of the Senate, Banda cited the need to curb and protect Nigerians from destructive and foreign moral influence. Same-sex marriage is currently not legal in Nigeria, as Nigerian law recognizes three classes of marriage: Christian or statutory, customary and Islamic. None of these systems of matrimonial law countenances marriages between persons of the same sex. Additionally, Nigerian law already criminalizes homosexual conduct, making it even harder to justify the introduction of the present bill. This is evidenced in the provisions of the penal code law applicable in all the states in northern Nigeria and the criminal code laws of all the states in southern Nigeria. For example, see section 284 of the penal code law and sections 214, 217 and 227 of the criminal code law. The sharia law, widely practiced in most parts of northern Nigeria, provides for sentences including the death penalty for homosexual offenses. . . . The criminal code law and the penal code law have been in force since 1945 and 1968 respectively, while the sharia codes have been in force for about 10 years in most parts of northern Nigeria. This again brings into question the rationale for the new law, especially since no person or group has ever raised the issue of their desire to engage in same-sex marriage.

It will be inappropriate to attempt any discussion of this bill without addressing some of the religious and cultural concerns of its promoters. It is instructive to note that the proponents of the bill said that homosexuality is "un-African," yet they turn to Christianity, a religion that is not African, and is indeed opposed to several African traditions, to explain their point. Further, Nigerian jurisprudence has a long history of separating the institution of religion from the law. Aside from these points, it must also be pointed out that this bill has grave implications for individual rights of the people and democracy in Nigeria.

Same-sex marriage is currently not legal in Nigeria.

Violations of National and International Rights

The bill would have a devastating effect on a range of civil society organizations in Nigeria while inciting hatred and violence against anyone suspected of practicing or supporting same-sex relationships, including but not limited to LGBT [lesbian, gay, bisexual, and transgender] persons and activists.

It is frightening in its possibilities for doing great damage to the fundamental rights of citizens. The provisions of the bill are in clear violation of the Nigerian Constitution and international instruments to which Nigeria is a state party.

Provisions in the bill violate sections 37, 38, 40 and 42 of Nigeria's Constitution, and the analogous provisions of the African Charter on Human and Peoples' Rights (articles 2, 3, 11 and 28) and the International Covenant on Civil and Political Rights (ICCPR) (articles 2, 18, 19, 21, 22 and 26). The Constitution of the Federal Republic of Nigeria, 1999, guarantees certain fundamental rights to all citizens in chapter IV. Section 34 guarantees the right to the dignity of the human person. Section 34 expressly forbids discrimination on the ground of sex, race, color, language, religion, political or other opinion, national and social origin, fortune, birth or other status.

Although the UN [United Nations] Human Rights Committee established in *Joslin v. New Zealand* that the ICCPR does not recognize a fundamental right to marry for same-sex couples under article 23(2), in *Young v. Australia* the committee did recognize that differential treatment between unmarried same-sex and different-sex couples may constitute a breach of state party obligations under the prohibition of discrimination in article 26.

The provisions of the bill are in clear violation of the Nigerian Constitution and international instruments to which Nigeria is a state party.

Implications of the Bill

Section 5(3) of the bill, which attempts to criminalize anybody who "witnesses, aids or abets the solemnization of same-sex union," is very problematic as it introduces widespread censorship and undermines fundamental freedoms such as speech, expression, association and assembly.

Sections 37, 38, 40, and 42 of the Nigerian Constitution

37. The privacy of citizens, their homes, correspondence, telephone conversations and telegraphic communications is hereby guaranteed and protected.

38. (1) Every person shall be entitled to freedom of thought, conscience and religion, including freedom to change his religion or belief, and freedom . . . to manifest and propagate his religion or belief in worship, teaching, practice and observance. . . .

40. Every person shall be entitled to assemble freely and associate with other persons, and in particular he may form or belong to any political party, trade union or any other association for the protection of his interests. . . .

42. (1) A citizen of Nigeria of a particular community, ethnic group, place of origin, sex, religion or political opinion shall not, by reason only that he is such a person:

(a) be subjected either expressly by, or in the practical application of, any law in force in Nigeria or any executive or administrative action of the government, to disabilities or restrictions to which citizens of Nigeria of other communities, ethnic groups, places of origin, sex, religions or political opinions are not made subject; or

(b) be accorded either expressly by, or in the practical application of, any law in force in Nigeria or any such executive or administrative action, any privilege or advantage that is not accorded to citizens of Nigeria of other communities, ethnic groups, places of origin, sex, religions or political opinions.

"Chapter IV: Fundamental Rights,"
Constitution of the Federal Republic of Nigeria, 1999.

The bill is clearly discriminatory as it singles out one group of people to be deprived of rights that all people enjoy as guaranteed by the Constitution and international human rights treaties to which Nigeria is a state party. In particular, the bill violates the right to freedom from discrimination as recognized in section 42(1) of the Nigerian Constitution.

The potential political implications are equally enormous. Opposition politicians and activists can simply be labeled as homosexuals to ensure that they are discredited. A case in point was in January 2011, during the presidential primaries of the ruling Peoples Democratic Party (PDP).

Opponents of former vice president Alhaji Atiku Abubakar assembled a group of young men under the banner of "Nigerian Gay Forum," purportedly seeking voter support for Atiku, because "he is one of us."

The provisions of the bill are vague in their most dangerous places and the enforcement of the law is left to the subjective opinion of the enforcers. The provisions of section 5(2), for instance, prohibit publicity, procession and public shows of gay relationships. The danger in this provision is that it is a license for the enforcers of the law to determine what amounts to a public show of an amorous relationship.

A Violation of Rights

The UN Human Rights Committee has consistently argued that any domestic law criminalizing private, same-sex behavior between consenting adults is a violation of the principle of nondiscrimination. See, for instance, the observations delivered with reference to Egypt in 2002, Ecuador in 1998, and the US in 1995 and 2006. It should be noted that Nigeria acceded to the ICCPR without reservations in 1993. On the authority of *Toonen v. Australia*, the committee made far-reaching pronouncements on the issue of discrimination on the basis of sexual orientation and held that states cannot curtail human rights on the basis of sexual orientation. The same-sex marriage bill is a clear negation of duty of the Nigerian state, which is a state party to the ICCPR and other international instruments prohibiting discrimination on the basis of sexual orientation.

The provisions of the bill are vague in their most dangerous places and the enforcement of the law is left to the subjective opinion of the enforcers.

Section 45 of the Nigerian Constitution has placed restrictions on some of the fundamental rights guaranteed in sections 36, 38, 39, 40 and 41, in the interest of defense, public safety, public order, public morality or public health; or for the purpose of protecting the rights and freedoms of other persons. It is worthy to note that the right to freedom from discrimination is not included in the restrictions. Even if section 42 had been included, the bill would still not have been covered, as it would have been against the interest of public health and the behavior being criminalized cannot be said to infringe on the rights of others. Public morality cannot also be in issue with respect to consensual relationship in private.

The Nigerian Constitution equally guarantees the right to privacy and family life in section 37. This right is to protect the privacy of the citizen at home as well as his correspondence; section 5(3) of this bill is a clear violation of this right. Under the guise of enforcing this law, the state can violate the citizen's right to privacy with impunity.

Dangers of the Bill

If passed into law, the bill will amount to an incitement to persecute persons on the basis of their sexual orientation. Article 7 of the Universal Declaration of Human Rights prohibits any incitements to discrimination; the present bill will act as a license for torture and ill treatment based on sexual orientation. By institutionalizing discrimination, the law will act as an official incitement to violence against lesbians and gay men in the community as a whole, whether in custody, in prison, on the street or in the home. Additionally, the bill will deprive gays and lesbians the right to life by obstructing access to HIV/AIDS programs, as it is capable of driving people already suffering stigma for their sexual identity still further underground. Clearly it is wrong to prevent persons from accessing medical facilities on the basis of their sexual orientation. If it becomes impossible under the legal regime for the gay community to access medical facilities, or if they cannot be beneficiaries of the HIV prevention and campaign efforts, this amounts to a violation of the right to life guaranteed under section 33 of the Constitution.

The Nigerian government needs to rise up to fulfill its fundamental obligations and responsibilities to its entire citizenry and to overturn this colossal human rights violation.

The bill will also open avenues for human rights violations by the Nigerian police even among heterosexual individuals, including thousands of migrant workers and students who share rooms in major Nigerian cities for economic reasons. In the wake of a similar bill in 2007, security men forced their way into a party and arrested 18 young men in August 2007 in Bauchi, northern Nigeria. They were later charged with organizing gay marriages. Also expected to increase is the practice of police and vigilantes breaking into hotel rooms, seeking out gay couples.

This discourse merely attempts to highlight the dangers of the bill and its implication for Nigeria's democratic process. The same-sex marriage bill is offensive, discriminatory and a violation of ICCPR and the Yogyakarta Principles, among other human rights treaties. Above all, the Nigerian government needs to rise up to fulfill its fundamental obligations and responsibilities to its entire citizenry and to overturn this colossal human rights violation, and protect the rights and dignity of all, including sexual minorities.

The Constitutional Dimensions of the Same-Sex Marriage Debate

Pew Research Center

In the following viewpoint, Pew Research Center contends thats the US legal battles concerning same-sex marriage being waged at the state and federal levels are rooted partly in the question of whether state and federal constitutions protect a right to privacy. The authors recount how the right to privacy developed in the US Supreme Court, finding antisodomy laws unconstitutional because of the violation of the right to privacy. The authors claim that the court's reasoning in previous privacy cases has been used by state courts to support same-sex marriage and such reasoning may end up being used by the US Supreme Court. The report was written by David Masci, senior research fellow, and Jesse Merriam, research associate, at Pew Research Center's Forum on Religion and Public Life. Pew Research Center is a nonpartisan think tank that informs the public about the issues, attitudes, and trends shaping America and the world. It conducts public opinion polling, demographic research, media content analysis, and other empirical social science research.

Pew Research Center, "The Constitutional Dimensions of the Same-Sex Marriage Debate," Pew Forum on Religion and Public Life, July 9, 2009. Copyright © 2009, http://www.pewforum.org/2008/04/01/the-constitutional-dimensions-of-the-same-sex -marriage-debate-2008/.

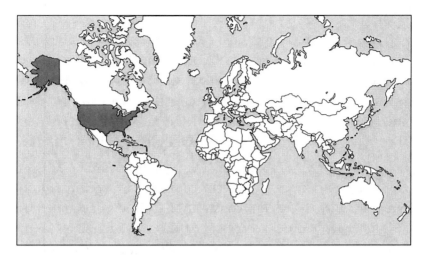

As you read, consider the following questions:

1. According to Pew Research Center, which US Supreme Court case first identified a right to marital privacy?

2. At the time of the court's decision in *Lawrence v. Texas* (2003), how many states had antisodomy laws that were enforced, according to Pew Research Center?

3. Pew Research Center claims that in 2006 and 2007 the highest courts in which three states determined that their state constitutions do not guarantee same-sex couples the right to marry?

On May 21, 2009, the California Supreme Court closed another chapter in the state's long-running fight over same-sex marriage when it upheld a 2008 voter-approved ballot initiative, known as Proposition 8, which amended the California state constitution to ban gay marriage. A month earlier, on April 27, 2009, the Iowa Supreme Court had unanimously ruled that a state law defining marriage solely as a union between a man and a woman violated the Iowa Constitution's guarantee of equal protection. (See A Contentious Debate: Same-Sex Marriage in the U.S.)

As the California and Iowa rulings suggest, while the gay marriage controversy has many elements, including disagreements over religious and social norms, much of the debate is a legal one. Indeed, it was a 2003 Massachusetts high court decision legalizing same-sex marriage that elevated the issue onto the national stage, where it has remained ever since. Since 2003, courts in a number of states have handed victories to both opponents and supporters of gay marriage.

So far, court cases around the country have been based on state, rather than federal, constitutional provisions and thus have not been subject to review by the U.S. Supreme Court. However, a suit alleging that California's Proposition 8 violates the U.S. Constitution was recently filed in a federal district court, giving the nation's high court a potential opportunity to determine whether the U.S Constitution guarantees the right of gay and lesbian couples to wed. If the court takes such a case, its decision will likely stem, at least in part, from its prior rulings on privacy and related issues.

The Right to Privacy and the *Griswold* Revolution

Although the legal battle over same-sex marriage is rooted, in part, in the question of whether state and federal constitutions protect a right to privacy, the word "privacy" never actually appears in the U.S. Constitution. However, the Constitution does recognize several rights relating to privacy. For example, the Fourth Amendment recognizes the importance of privacy interests when it stipulates that because citizens need to feel "secure in their persons, houses, papers and effects," the government may not carry out "unreasonable searches and seizures." In addition, the Ninth Amendment leaves open the possibility of a broader privacy right when it declares that there are rights "retained by the people" that do not expressly appear in the Bill of Rights.

The Supreme Court first laid the foundation for an expanded right to privacy early in the 20th century in *Lochner v. New York* (1905). In this case, the court relied on the reference to "liberty" in the 14th Amendment's due process clause, which states that no person "shall be deprived of life, liberty or property, without due process of law," to justify striking down a New York state law limiting the number of hours bakers could work each week. According to the court majority, the due process clause implicitly guarantees citizens the "fundamental" right, free from state intrusion, to enter into employment arrangements.

The Constitution does recognize several rights relating to privacy.

The court's reasoning in *Lochner* animated many subsequent decisions that form the foundation of what today is known as the constitutional right to privacy. In one such decision, *Pierce v. Society of Sisters* (1925), the court ruled that an Oregon law banning all private education violated the due process clause because it directed how parents may educate their children, infringing upon parents' fundamental right to rear their children as they see fit. In his majority opinion, Justice James Clark McReynolds went on to list other rights guaranteed by the due process clause, including "the right of the individual . . . to marry, establish a home and bring up children . . . and generally to enjoy those privileges long recognized at common law as essential to the orderly pursuit of happiness by free men."

Four decades later, in *Griswold v. Connecticut* (1965), the Supreme Court again turned its attention to whether the Constitution implicitly contains fundamental privacy guarantees. In this case, the court held by a vote of 7-2 that a Connecticut law prohibiting the sale and use of birth control was unconstitutional because it intruded on the right of marital privacy.

Writing for the majority, Justice William O. Douglas asserted that a right to privacy exists not because of a specific constitutional provision but rather because it flows from several provisions relating to privacy, such as the Third Amendment right to refuse to quarter soldiers during peacetime and the Fourth Amendment prohibition of unreasonable searches and seizures. These and other privacy-related provisions, Justice Douglas wrote, create "penumbras" (or shadows) in which "zones of privacy" exist. Within these zones, he declared, are other rights, including the right of married couples to determine whether or not to have children.

In their dissent, Justices Potter Stewart and Hugo Black, while agreeing with the majority that the Connecticut statute was "an uncommonly silly law," explained that they would have upheld the law because the Constitution does not speak to a general right to privacy. Both justices expressed a fear that the majority's focus on constitutional penumbras would lead to judicial overreaching. "The adoption of such a loose, flexible, uncontrolled standard for holding laws unconstitutional, if ever it is finally achieved, will amount to a great unconstitutional shift of power to the courts, which I believe . . . will be bad for the courts and worse for the country," Justice Black wrote.

Echoes of *Griswold* could be heard two years later in *Loving v. Virginia* (1967), a famous case involving a challenge to a Virginia law banning interracial marriage. In a unanimous decision, the court ruled that this law violated the 14th Amendment's equal protection clause, which guarantees all citizens equal protection under the law and thus prohibits the government from discriminating on the basis of race. But the court moved beyond the issue of racial discrimination to assert that the right to marry is itself protected by the Constitution. "The freedom to marry has long been recognized as one of the vital personal rights essential to the orderly pursuit of happiness by free men," wrote Chief Justice Earl Warren for the majority. "Marriage is one of the 'basic civil rights of man,' fundamental to our very existence and survival," the chief justice added.

Justice William O. Douglas asserted that a right to privacy exists not because of a specific constitutional provision but rather because it flows from several provisions relating to privacy.

In *Eisenstadt v. Baird* (1972), the court broadened the right to privacy enunciated in *Griswold* to include unmarried people. This case involved a Massachusetts law prohibiting the distribution of birth control to single people. By a vote of 6-1 (there were two vacancies on the court at the time), the court struck down the law. "If the right of privacy means anything," Justice William Brennan wrote, "it is the right of the individual, married or single, to be free from unwarranted governmental intrusion into matters so fundamentally affecting a person as the decision whether to bear or beget a child."

The following year the court extended privacy rights even further when, in *Roe v. Wade* (1973), it established a constitutional right to abortion. Writing for the majority, Justice Harry Blackmun explained that the "right of privacy . . . founded in the 14th Amendment's concept of personal liberty and restrictions upon state action is broad enough to encompass a woman's decision whether or not to terminate her pregnancy." The court thus returned to locating the right to privacy in the due process clause.

Starting in the 1970s, some politicians and legal thinkers began arguing that the court's privacy jurisprudence, particularly as articulated in *Griswold* and *Roe*, amounted to judicial activism by creating rights that were never envisioned in the Constitution. Although this critique was most popular in conservative circles, it also won over some liberals and moderates who feared a significant expansion of the Supreme Court's power. In response to this criticism, some legal scholars countered that the *Griswold* and *Roe* decisions were logical outgrowths of a long line of the court's decisions and were therefore harmonious with the court's tradition of enforcing fundamental rights that are not directly specified in the Constitution.

The Gay Rights Movement and the Road to *Lawrence*

During the 1970s, a gay rights movement, patterned in many ways after the civil rights and women's rights movements, developed momentum as the sexual revolution spurred new social and sexual mores, which in turn prompted legislatures to repeal many state laws regulating sexuality. For instance, some 20 states, including California and Ohio, struck from the books their anti-sodomy laws. Still, by the mid-1980s, laws that prohibited certain acts between people of the same sex, and in some cases between those of the opposite sex, remained in force in 25 states.

One of these state laws, a Georgia anti-sodomy statute, became the subject of a landmark high court ruling. The case, *Bowers v. Hardwick* (1986), arose after Atlanta police arrested Michael Hardwick for having consensual sex in his own bedroom with another man. Georgia, like most states, rarely enforced its anti-sodomy law and, indeed, the state eventually dropped its charges against Hardwick. Nevertheless, Hardwick sued the state, alleging that the criminalization of private and consensual sex between people of the same gender violated his constitutional right to privacy.

In a 5-4 ruling, a bitterly divided Supreme Court ruled that the constitutional right to privacy did not protect the right to have private, consensual sex with a person of the same gender. Writing for the majority, Justice Byron White declared that earlier privacy cases, such as *Griswold* and *Loving*, concerned "family, marriage or procreation." It would be an untenable stretch, White reasoned, to extend privacy rights to "any kind of private sexual conduct between consenting adults." Furthermore, he wrote, while existing privacy protections concerning marriage or child rearing "are deeply rooted in this nation's history and tradition," the opposite was true of sodomy, which all states had at one time banned and which half the states still banned at the time of the decision.

One of these state laws, a Georgia anti-sodomy statute, became the subject of a landmark high court ruling.

In a strongly worded dissent, Justice Blackmun dismissed the majority's contention that the case ultimately involved a "fundamental right to engage in homosexual sodomy." Indeed, he accused the majority of "distort[ing]" the ultimate question before the court by ignoring the fact that the Georgia statute outlawed sodomy between heterosexuals as well as homosexuals. What the case actually concerned, Justice Blackmun wrote, was "the most comprehensive of rights and the right most valued by civilized men, namely, the right to be let alone." More specifically, he argued, the Constitution guarantees each person, regardless of sexual orientation, the liberty to have consensual intimate relations in his or her own home.

Many conservatives hailed the *Bowers* decision as a much-needed restraint on a court that they said had become untethered from its constitutional mandate. But a hint of change in course came just four years after the ruling, when Justice Lewis Powell, who had provided the crucial fifth vote for the *Bowers* majority, stated publicly that he subsequently regretted his decision. "I think I probably made a mistake," he admitted, three years after retiring from the bench.

Meanwhile, in 1996 the high court decided *Romer v. Evans*, an important gay rights ruling that, while addressing a different question than the *Bowers* case, ultimately proved to be a strong indicator of how the court might rule if it revisited the sodomy question. In the *Romer* case, the court considered a challenge to an amendment to the Colorado Constitution (approved by the state's voters in 1992) that nullified local anti-discrimination protections for homosexuals and prohibited passage of any such anti-discrimination laws in the future. By a 6-3 vote, the high court held that the Colorado amendment violated the 14th Amendment guarantee of equal protection. "A state cannot so deem a class of persons a stranger to its laws," wrote Justice Anthony Kennedy in the majority opinion. In particular, he found, "the [Colorado] amendment imposes a special disability upon [homosexuals]," who are "forbidden the safeguards that others enjoy or may seek without restraint."

While Justice Kennedy did not specifically mention *Bowers*, Justice Antonin Scalia, in a forceful dissent, reasoned that the *Bowers* decision should have led the court to uphold the Colorado law. "If it is rational to criminalize the conduct," he wrote, referring to the Georgia sodomy statute upheld in *Bowers*, "surely it is rational to deny special favor and protection to those with a self-avowed tendency or desire to engage in the conduct."

The *Lawrence* Case and Scalia's Dissent

As if in response to Justice Scalia's dissent in *Romer*, the court soon revisited the issue it had decided in *Bowers*, taking up another challenge to a sodomy statute, this one from Texas. The case, *Lawrence v. Texas* (2003), is remarkably similar to *Bowers* in many of its facts. Once again, police discovered two men having consensual sex in a private residence and arrested them under a state anti-sodomy law. And, once again, the defendants challenged the sodomy statute's constitutionality, taking the case all the way to the Supreme Court.

Despite these factual similarities, the court in *Lawrence* overruled its earlier decision in *Bowers*, thereby invalidating not only the Texas statute but all anti-sodomy laws. Writing for the majority, Justice Kennedy stated that the court in *Bow-*

State Politics on Same-Sex Marriage

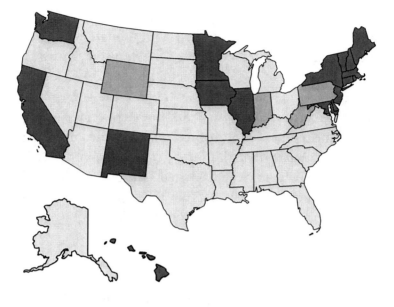

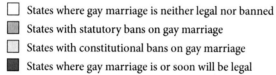

☐ States where gay marriage is neither legal nor banned
▨ States with statutory bans on gay marriage
☐ States with constitutional bans on gay marriage
■ States where gay marriage is or soon will be legal

TAKEN FROM: Pew Forum on Religion and Public Life, "Same-Sex Marriage State-by-State," January 2014.

ers had been mistaken in concluding that the government had historically restricted private and consensual intimate relations between people of the same sex. Moreover, Kennedy explained, sexual mores had changed since *Bowers*, as evidenced by the fact that in the 17 years between the *Bowers* and *Lawrence* cases, 12 states had repealed their anti-sodomy statutes and nine stopped enforcing these laws, leaving only four states that continued to enforce them.

Finally, Kennedy wrote, gay people have a "liberty under the due process clause [that] gives them the full right to engage in [intimate] conduct without intervention of the government." No matter how unpopular a group's sexual norms, he explained, the government may not "demean their existence or control their destiny by making their private sexual conduct a crime." In making this claim, though, Kennedy was quick to note the limited breadth of the decision. This case, he assured, did not address the regulation of prostitution or other public sexual acts, nor did it require the government to extend marriage or civil unions to same-sex couples.

Just as he did in *Romer*, Justice Scalia dissented in *Lawrence*, arguing once again that the majority's reassurances did not agree with their logic. Scalia asserted that by rejecting moral-based legislation, Kennedy and the other justices on the majority were paving the way for a future ruling requiring states to recognize same-sex unions.

The Massachusetts Decision

Ironically, Justice Scalia's interpretation of the *Lawrence* majority opinion would prove to have a profound effect on the gay rights movement. Many lawyers subsequently arguing for a right to same-sex marriage pointed to Scalia's dissent in *Lawrence* as evidence that the majority opinion in that case generated a constitutional right to marriage for people of the same gender.

The court in Lawrence *overruled its earlier decision in* Bowers, *thereby invalidating not only the Texas statute but all anti-sodomy laws.*

Previously, in the 1990s, supreme courts in Hawaii and Vermont interpreted their respective state constitutions to require that their state governments offer same-sex couples the same rights and benefits of marriage afforded to opposite-sex couples, even if the state chose not to define these rights and benefits as marriage. In response, many states, fearing that their courts would issue similar decisions, passed what are known collectively as defense of marriage acts (DOMAs), which specifically define marriage as a union between an opposite-sex couple. In addition, several states amended their constitutions to prohibit same-sex marriage, hoping that such an explicit ban would prevent their courts from reading other constitutional provisions so broadly as to guarantee same-sex couples the right to marry.

Despite the creation of DOMAs and other state legislative actions preceding *Lawrence*, the *Lawrence* decision dramatically changed the same-sex marriage landscape by articulating a constitutional framework that could provide robust rights for gay and lesbian couples. Indeed, echoes of *Lawrence* could be heard in *Goodridge v. Department of Public Health* (2003), a decision by the Massachusetts high court that ignited a national debate over the meaning of marriage.

Several states amended their constitutions to prohibit same-sex marriage, hoping that such an explicit ban would prevent their courts from reading other constitutional provisions so broadly as to guarantee same-sex couples the right to marry.

In *Goodridge*, the Massachusetts Supreme Judicial Court held by a vote of 4-3 that the state's constitution requires the government to offer "the protections, benefits and obligations conferred by civil marriage to two individuals of the same sex who wish to marry." The case arose after Julie and Hillary Goodridge, a lesbian couple, sought a marriage license from the Massachusetts Department of Health. The department denied the request, claiming that Massachusetts did not recognize same-sex marriage. The Goodridges then sued the department, alleging that this denial violated their right to individual liberty and legal equality as guaranteed by the Massachusetts Constitution.

Writing for the majority, Chief Justice Margaret Marshall held that denying marriage benefits to same-sex couples violated the Massachusetts Constitution because it did not accomplish a legitimate government goal. Indeed, the court explained, the reasons the government offered for banning same-sex marriage—promoting procreation, ensuring a good child-rearing environment and preserving state financial resources—would not be promoted by prohibiting same-sex couples from marrying. Thus, according to the court, the only basis for the state's decision to exclude same-sex couples from the institution of marriage was a disapproval of their lifestyle. Because the court concluded that condemning a lifestyle is not a "constitutionally adequate reason" for denying marriage benefits, it held that the state must permit same-sex couples to marry.

In contrast, the three dissenting judges in *Goodridge* argued that they would not have required the state to recognize such unions because the state legislature enjoys broad discretion when regulating nonfundamental rights, such as the right to same-sex marriage. Given this discretion, the dissenting judges argued, the court should be very deferential in determining whether there is a connection between the ban on same-sex marriage and the legislature's asserted interests. Applying this level of deference, the dissenting judges concluded that the legislature had a rational basis for two of its three stated purposes in banning same-sex marriage: to communicate to its citizens the view that marriage is about procreation and to promote the optimal setting for rearing children.

Then-governor of Massachusetts Mitt Romney responded to the *Goodridge* decision by proposing to amend the Massachusetts Constitution to define marriage as a union between one man and one woman. Under Massachusetts law, the legislature must approve a constitutional amendment in two consecutive sessions before the people can vote on it. After fighting a long and contentious battle over Romney's proposal, the legislature approved a compromise amendment in 2004 that prohibited gay marriage but created civil unions for same-sex couples. In the following session, however, the legislature changed course and rejected this proposed amendment, thus denying voters the opportunity to consider it.

The Growing Battle Over Same-Sex Marriage in the States

Meanwhile, a debate over same-sex marriage was heating up at both the federal and state levels. Many states became concerned that the U.S. Constitution's full faith and credit clause, which generally requires states to enforce judicial decisions issued in other states, would require each state to recognize a marriage between same-sex partners that took place in Massachusetts. Many scholars have noted that this is probably an unfounded concern since the Supreme Court held many years ago that states need not violate their own policy interests in enforcing other states' policies on marriage. In addition, the federal Defense of Marriage Act, which was signed into law by President Bill Clinton in 1996, explicitly exempts states from having to recognize a same-sex marriage legally performed in another state.

Nevertheless, in 2003, 2004 and 2006, opponents of gay marriage in the U.S. Congress found this concern serious enough to declare it as the principal basis for proposing an amendment to the U.S. Constitution banning same-sex marriage in every state. This effort, however, failed to receive the two-thirds majority of both the U.S. House of Representatives and the U.S. Senate required to send a proposed federal constitutional amendment to the states for ratification.

At the state level, the success of the plaintiffs in *Goodridge* inspired other gay and lesbian couples to file similar claims around the country. Until May 2008, however, only one of these cases, *Lewis v. Harris* (2006), was even partly successful. In that case, the New Jersey Supreme Court found that the state constitutional guarantee of legal equality required the state legislature to grant same-sex couples the same rights and benefits of marriage that opposite-sex couples have traditionally enjoyed. Although important, the *Lewis* decision did not match the breadth of *Goodridge* because the court permitted the state lawmakers to decide how to grant these rights—either by marriage or civil union. Soon after the ruling, the New Jersey legislature passed a measure allowing gay and lesbian couples to enter into civil unions but not to marry.

Besides the New Jersey decision, all of the suits on this subject at the state supreme court level were unsuccessful until May 2008. Indeed, in 2006 and 2007, the highest courts in New York, Washington and Maryland found that their state constitutions do not guarantee same-sex couples the right to marry. Each of these decisions held that recognizing same-sex marriage is a policy matter, not a constitutional matter, and that the decision must therefore rest with the people's representatives in the legislative and executive branches.

Proposition 8 and the Battle in California

In May 2008, the California Supreme Court held 4-3 that state laws limiting marriage to opposite-sex couples violated the state constitution. The California decision, which consolidated six individual cases, is much like the *Goodridge* decision in that it found that same-sex couples are constitutionally entitled to the identical marital rights and privileges as opposite-sex couples. The reasoning in the *Goodridge* and California decisions, however, differed in one fundamental respect: Whereas the Massachusetts court in *Goodridge* found a right to same-sex marriage on the ground that there is no rational basis for denying marital rights to same-sex couples, the California court went significantly further, elevating gays and lesbians to have the same protected legal status as racial minorities and women. A law that discriminates against one of these protected groups is constitutional only if it meets a compelling government need. So the upshot of this ruling was that the California Constitution generally forbids any distinction whatsoever between same-sex and opposite-sex unions, whether in benefits or merely in name.

Seeking to overrule this decision, same-sex marriage opponents placed Proposition 8, a measure to alter the California Constitution to ban gay marriage, on the November 2008 state ballot. Following expensive and contentious political campaigns waged by both supporters and opponents of the initiative, California voters passed the proposition by a narrow margin—effectively outlawing gay marriage in California.

But just one day after the passage of the initiative, same-sex marriage advocates filed a lawsuit in the California Supreme Court claiming that Proposition 8 was not constitutionally valid and thus did not trump the California high court's earlier ruling that the state must recognize the right to same-sex marriage. The legal basis for the lawsuit was that California law provides for two types of changes to the state constitution: revisions and amendments. A revision is a "substantial" change to the constitution; it requires a vote by at least two-thirds of both houses of the California legislature to submit the proposed revision to a popular vote or to a constitutional convention. An amendment is a less substantial change to the constitution that only requires voters to place the proposed amendment on a state ballot and win a majority vote, as Californians did with Proposition 8. Gay-rights advocates argued that because the right of gays and lesbians to wed is a fundamental right, banning the practice required a constitutional revision, not just an amendment. Therefore, these advocates asserted, Proposition 8 was invalid.

On May 26, 2009, the California Supreme Court ruled 6-1 that Proposition 8 was an amendment, not a revision, and thus was valid. In its decision, the court noted that constitutional revision generally entails a significant change to the state's governmental framework, something Proposition 8 does not do. In addition, the majority noted, earlier ballot initiatives that had altered fundamental constitutional rights—such as the restoration of the state's death penalty in 1972—had also been deemed to be amendments, not revisions.

After upholding Proposition 8, the court turned its attention to the status of the 18,000 gay and lesbian couples who had legally wed during the roughly five-month period between the May 2008 high court decision legalizing same-sex marriage and the early November passage of the proposition banning it. Here the court sided with gay marriage advocates, ruling that the marriages would remain valid because the language of Proposition 8 does not explicitly apply the ban retroactively.

Finally, the court noted that those same-sex couples could still achieve the material benefits and obligations of marriage under California law thanks to the court's May 2008 decision legalizing the practice. Proposition 8 did not "repeal or abrogate" these rights, wrote Chief Justice Ronald M. George for the majority. Instead, George added, Proposition 8 merely carved "out a narrow and limited exception to these state constitutional rights, reserving the official designation of the term 'marriage' for the union of opposite-sex couples." Furthermore, the other major piece of the May decision—making gays and lesbians a protected class in future discrimination cases—also continues to stand.

Connecticut and Iowa Legalize Gay Marriage

Gay marriage advocates counted the Proposition 8 decision as a major defeat, but they did score important victories around the same time in two other state high courts. The first of these wins occurred in October 2008, in the Connecticut Supreme Court. In *Kerrigan v. Connecticut Department of Health* (2008), the state's high court ruled by a vote of 4-3 that a state law banning same-sex marriage violated the state constitution's guarantee of equal protection under the law.

The ruling overturned an earlier decision by a Connecticut trial court that had found no violation of the state's equal protection clause because the state had enacted a civil union law giving gay and lesbian couples the same legal rights as married couples. In this earlier decision, the trial court judge had written that the state constitution requires equal protection under the law but "not that there be equivalent nomenclature for such protection."

But the majority of the Connecticut Supreme Court disagreed, ruling that offering homosexual couples civil unions in lieu of marriage amounts to unequal treatment "because the institution of marriage carries with it a status and significance that the newly created classification of civil unions does not embody." In addition, the Connecticut Supreme Court elevated the legal status of gays and lesbians, giving them greater protection against discrimination than was granted in the Massachusetts decision, but not the highest level of protection that was established in the California ruling. In *Kerrigan*, the Connecticut high court ruled that laws that discriminate against gays and lesbians must be subjected to what is known as "intermediate strict scrutiny." This means that a law that discriminates against homosexuals will be struck down unless the state can show that it substantially furthers an important government interest.

Five months after the Connecticut decision, the Iowa Supreme Court followed suit, unanimously affirming a lower court ruling that struck down the state's 1998 DOMA banning same-sex marriage. The decision shocked many observers because Iowa is a Midwestern state with a substantial population of Christian social conservatives. However, the state also has long been known for its populist tradition and its willingness to embrace socially liberal causes.

As in Connecticut, the justices in the Iowa case struck down the law on the grounds that it violated the state constitution's equal protection clause. And, as in Connecticut, the court in Iowa established the "intermediate strict scrutiny" test when assessing laws—including the DOMA—that discriminate against gays and lesbians, meaning that these laws can only be upheld if they substantially further an important government interest. In this case, the court ruled, Iowa's DOMA did "not substantially further any government objective" and was thus unconstitutional.

Looking Ahead

Gay rights advocates will almost certainly continue to file lawsuits at the state level. In addition, two prominent lawyers from opposite sides of the ideological fence have moved the issue into the federal court system. Former solicitor general Ted Olson and high-profile litigator David Boies, the two lawyers who faced off against each other in the famed Supreme Court case *Bush v. Gore* (2000), have joined forces and filed a suit in federal district court in San Francisco arguing that Proposition 8 violates the equal protection and due process clauses of the U.S. Constitution. Olson and Boies have publicly predicted that their case will end up before the U.S. Supreme Court, although such a result is by no means assured.

Still, filing such a claim at the federal level poses some risks for the gay marriage movement. An unfavorable outcome for same-sex marriage supporters in the U.S. Supreme Court would prevent gay couples from subsequently arguing for a right to same-sex marriage under the U.S. Constitution; gay couples would be able to secure a right to marriage only under state constitutions. Moreover, an unfavorable high court ruling might influence the judgment of state courts in future gay marriage decisions. Because of such concerns, a number of prominent gay rights groups, such as the Human Rights Campaign and Lambda Legal, have publicly questioned the decision by Olson and Boies to file the suit, arguing that such a case may be premature or even dangerous to the success of the same-sex marriage movement.

While it is impossible to predict how the high court might rule in a same-sex marriage case, several of the justices' past decisions offer some clues. Of all the justices, Justices Scalia and Clarence Thomas probably offer the most solid indicators as to how they might rule. Indeed, given their dissenting opinions in *Lawrence*, it would be surprising if either justice voted for a constitutional right to same-sex marriage. At the same time, it is more difficult to predict the votes of their two conservative colleagues, Chief Justice John Roberts and Justice Samuel Alito, because Roberts and Alito were not on the court when earlier gay rights cases, such as *Lawrence*, were decided. However, many constitutional scholars predict that Roberts and Alito would most likely join Scalia and Thomas on this issue.

An unfavorable outcome for same-sex marriage supporters in the U.S. Supreme Court would prevent gay couples from subsequently arguing for a right to same-sex marriage under the U.S. Constitution.

The court's more liberal justices, Stephen Breyer, Ruth Bader Ginsburg and John Paul Stevens, have voted in favor of gay rights claimants in every gay rights case they have considered. However, these prior decisions, including *Lawrence*, never explicitly addressed whether the Constitution guarantees the right to gay marriage, making it difficult to know exactly how these justices might ultimately vote in a same-sex marriage case.

Like Roberts and Alito, federal judge Sonia Sotomayor—recently nominated by President Barack Obama to replace retired justice David Souter—has had no role in any major gay rights cases, and thus leaves few clues as to her likely vote in a case involving the constitutionality of same-sex marriage. However, many Supreme Court watchers predict that, if confirmed, Sotomayor would probably join the more liberal wing of the court on most, if not all, issues.

If conservatives and liberals on the court were to split 4-4 on the issue of same-sex marriage, the outcome in such a case would likely hinge on Justice Kennedy, whose vote can be difficult to predict. While Kennedy's opinion in *Lawrence* showed great sympathy for the gay rights movement, Kennedy also emphasized that, from a constitutional perspective, the case did "not involve whether the government must give formal recognition to any relationship that homosexual persons seek to enter." Kennedy thus explicitly refused to commit one way or the other on whether the Constitution requires recognition of same-sex marriages.

This report was written by David Masci, senior research fellow, and Jesse Merriam, research associate, Pew Research Center's Forum on Religion & Public Life.

Periodical and Internet Sources Bibliography

The following articles have been selected to supplement the diverse views presented in this chapter.

Amnesty International "Turkey: 'Not an Illness Nor a Crime': Lesbian, Gay, Bisexual and Transgender People in Turkey Demand Equality," June 21, 2011. www.amnesty.org.

Emily Cody "Uganda's Anti-Gay 'Christmas Gift,'" *Mantle* (blog), November 29, 2012. http://mantlethought.org.

Lyle Denniston "Same-Sex Marriage II: The Arguments For," *SCOTUSblog*, November 28, 2012. www.scotusblog.com.

Human Rights Watch "Malawi: Courageous Move to Suspend Anti-Gay Laws," November 6, 2012. www.hrw.org.

Bill Keller "Out in Africa," *New York Times*, December 23, 2012.

Christy Moore "Privacy Rights and Morality in a Tense Tango," *China Post* (Taiwan), November 24, 2012.

Siddharth Narrain "Sex, Lies and Videotape: The Right to Privacy in India," Infochange, March 2010. http://infochangeindia.org.

Robert O. Self "How Choice Won: Feminist Pioneers Built the Road to Roe with a Decades-Long Strategy Centered on Creating a Right to Privacy," *Salon*, September 22, 2012.

Mark Strasser "Same-Sex Marriage and the Right to Privacy," *Journal of Law and Family Studies*, vol. 13, 2011.

 **GLOBAL**VIEWPOINTS

 CHAPTER 4

Privacy and the Public Interest

In Ireland and the United Kingdom, Stronger Regulation of the Press Is Needed

Paul Tweed

In the following viewpoint, Paul Tweed argues that the fundamental right to privacy is at odds with the role of the press, creating questions about where to draw the line between respecting an individual's privacy and informing the public. Tweed contends that most proposals for reining in privacy violations by the tabloids are bound to fail, and he proposes that only new legislation can succeed in deterring the media from violating privacy. Tweed is a media lawyer specializing in defamation, privacy, piracy, and intellectual property issues. He is the author of Privacy and Libel Law: The Clash with Press Freedom.

As you read, consider the following questions:

1. According to the author, articles 8 and 10 of the European Convention on Human Rights require balancing of whose rights?
2. Tweed claims that the effectiveness of any new body charged with controlling the press will depend on what two factors?

Paul Tweed, "When Protection of Privacy and Rights of the Press Collide," *Irish Times*, April 16, 2012. Copyright © 2012 by Paul Tweed. All rights reserved. Republished with permission.

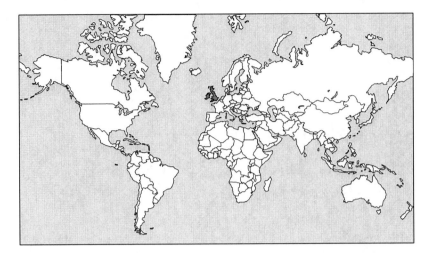

3. According to Tweed, editors face difficulty in balancing the individual's right to privacy with what other right?

Mark Twain once said: "There are laws to protect the freedom of the press's speech, but none that are worth anything to protect the people from the press."

The Fundamental Right to Privacy

While it is generally recognised that privacy is a fundamental human right, a more difficult question is whether that right can be diluted by an individual's conduct. What are the human rights of a politician who espouses family values to the electorate while carrying on an illicit affair? Does a newspaper have the right to publish such details, however sordid? What of the minor celebrity who co-ordinates shopping trips in the company of her children with paparazzi, in order that her carefully managed image will be splashed across the tabloid press? Does she have the right to subsequently object to unauthorised photographs being taken in a public place without her consent or connivance?

Possibly the broader question to be answered is whether our apparently insatiable appetite for celebrity and gossip has eroded our respect for the fundamental right to privacy, and this in turn has to be balanced against the role of the press in exposing corruption and hypocrisy in society. These questions represent only a few examples of conflicting issues and interests that require careful balancing in accordance with an individual's rights under article 8 of the European Convention on Human Rights and the article 10 rights of the press generally.

The daily dramas emerging from the Leveson Inquiry [a judicial public inquiry into the ethics of the press] in the UK [United Kingdom] have brought the issue of press regulation to the public's attention. With fallout over the hacking of the mobile phone of murdered schoolgirl Milly Dowler likely to continue for some time, with arrests and further disclosures on an almost weekly basis, the thorny issue of press regulation remains at the front of the agenda.

Many people . . . hold that only statutory regulation will be sufficient to ensure public confidence.

The Need for Greater Regulation

The general view is that the UK Press Complaints Commission had failed abysmally in its objective of controlling the greater excesses of the tabloid press in particular. Many suggested alternatives have been put on the table, from government, the legal profession, various interest groups and the press themselves, with suggestions ranging from a model based on the Press Ombudsman we have here in Ireland to more complex structures. However, the effectiveness of any new body will depend very much on the sanctions made available, and on the identity of those who will be given the task of adjudicating and implementing them.

Many people, including myself, hold that only statutory regulation will be sufficient to ensure public confidence. What

Articles 8 and 10 of the European Convention on Human Rights

Article 8

Right to respect for private and family life

1. Everyone has the right to respect for his private and family life, his home and his correspondence.

2. There shall be no interference by a public authority with the exercise of this right except such as is in accordance with the law and is necessary in a democratic society in the interests of national security, public safety or the economic well-being of the country. . . .

Article 10

Freedom of expression

1. Everyone has the right to freedom of expression. . . .

2. The exercise of these freedoms, since it carries with it duties and responsibilities, may be subject to such formalities, conditions, restrictions or penalties as are prescribed by law and are necessary in a democratic society. . . .

"Section 1: Rights and Freedoms,"
European Convention on Human Rights, 1953.

is required is an effective regulator that will operate in an impartial and independent manner, and, equally importantly, will be seen to do so.

The high cost of litigation and sometimes controversial remedies proposed by the courts, such as the "super injunction" (prohibiting information on the existence of an injunction), have been the subject of many column inches in the press. However, the first step in avoiding or reducing legal costs has to be the provision of an alternative in the form of a regulator with bite, or another form of adjudication that will produce vindication and, just as importantly, act as a deterrent to publication in the first place, and before the "privacy horse has bolted".

I believe investigative journalism should be protected where possible, but ask whether statutory regulation would in fact protect rather than stifle genuine investigative reporting.

Public Rights and Individual Privacy

Another question is whether there is an acceptable level of collateral damage to an individual's privacy which has to be tolerated to afford the press the freedom to uncover the genuine miscreants in our society.

Today's headlines are no longer tomorrow's fish and chip wrappers. With the Internet, any story in print or digital form will be quickly disseminated, tagged and repeated worldwide. One of the most difficult balances for any editor is between the right of the public to be told a story and the often conflicting rights relating to the individual's privacy.

As a lawyer acting for defamed individuals and defendant newspapers, I believe investigative journalism should be protected where possible, but ask whether statutory regulation would in fact protect rather than stifle genuine investigative reporting.

In the United States, Defamation and Invasion of Privacy Are Unchecked

Daniel J. Solove

In the following viewpoint, Daniel J. Solove argues that the decline in defamation lawsuits—such as libel lawsuits against media companies for the publication of disparaging comments—and privacy lawsuits are not the result of fewer problems with defamation and privacy invasion, but the result of a legal system that fails to adequately protect people from damaged reputations. Solove is the John Marshall Harlan Research Professor of Law at George Washington University and author of The Future of Reputation: Gossip, Rumor, and Privacy on the Internet *and* Nothing to Hide: The False Tradeoff Between Privacy and Security.

As you read, consider the following questions:

1. According to Solove, what percentage of defamation lawsuits are successful?
2. How have the courts interpreted section 230 of the Communications Decency Act, according to the author?
3. Solove claims that prior to the court system, people used what to vindicate their reputations?

Daniel J. Solove, "The Slow Demise of Defamation and the Privacy Torts," *Huffington Post*, October 11, 2010. Copyright © 2010 by Daniel J. Solove. All rights reserved. Republished with permission.

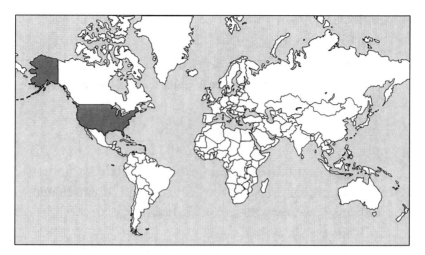

The *ABA Journal* reports that the number of libel suits has been steadily dropping in the United States:

> During his 30 years as a lawyer for the New York Times Co., George Freeman says, the "Gray Lady" faced four to five new libel suits per year, on average, and has had maybe eight pending against it at any one time. But that's all changed.
>
> Currently the *New York Times* is facing no libel suits, and the parent company faces just one in the U.S. "There's been a fairly steep decline" in the last few years, he says. "The real question is whether it's cyclical, as sometimes happens, although never quite to this degree, or whether there are other factors at play."
>
> The *Times* is definitely not alone, and the trend appears to have rolled out over two or three decades—not years— according to research from the Media Law Resource Center. The number of trials of libel, privacy and related claims against the media fell from 266 in the '80s to 192 in the '90s to 124 in the 2000s. In 2009, only nine such trials were held.

A Decline in Privacy Lawsuits

Why is this happening? Is it because there's much less defamation or invasion of privacy today? I strongly doubt that's the reason. Instead, I can think of several reasons for the decline in defamation and privacy trials:

1. Defamation lawsuits are very hard to win. Only about 13% are successful. It is thus hard to find lawyers who will take the case.

2. Invasion of privacy lawsuits are also hard to win. The privacy torts are fossilized into the forms they were in circa 1960, and they haven't evolved to address modern privacy problems. Moreover, courts cling to antiquated notions of privacy that make it hard for plaintiffs to prevail in a data-soaked world.

3. Focusing on trials might be the wrong thing to focus on. Trials themselves are becoming a rarity. Our legal system is overrun with costs, making it an extremely inefficient mechanism to resolve disputes. It is ridiculous that in many cases, the costs of litigating the suit can be greater than the actual money at stake in the lawsuit. Cases get settled just to avoid these costs.

4. Free speech has become exalted by courts in the past few decades. This is especially true with the Communications Decency Act Sec. 230, which courts have interpreted to immunize any ISP [Internet service provider] or website for comments made by their users—even when the ISP or website has knowledge the comments are defamatory or invasive of privacy and take no steps to do anything about it.

5. With social media, anybody now has the power to distribute information around the world. Much gossip and rumor now originates not in the mainstream media, but on Facebook, Myspace, blogs, and other forms of social media. By the time the mainstream media pick up a story, it has likely already been written about extensively online. For privacy cases, the people to sue are the ones who disclosed the information in the first place, and

they are likely to be people writing on social media websites. They often don't have deep pockets, so suing them isn't economically worthwhile.

6. When people bring suits for defamation and invasion of privacy, it is difficult for them to do so using a pseudonym. Courts have broad discretion about whether or not to let plaintiffs proceed under a pseudonym, and many courts are reluctant to allow people to do so. This has the effect of further publicizing the rumor or gossip. Thus, when a plaintiff tries to bring suit to clear away the information, it paradoxically results in increasing the dissemination of the information. For many plaintiffs, bringing a lawsuit might do more harm than good.

Courts cling to antiquated notions of privacy that make it hard for plaintiffs to prevail in a data-soaked world.

Methods for Protecting Reputations

I think this turn of events is unfortunate. People used to resort to self-help (violence and duels) to vindicate their reputations. Civilized society replaced these methods with a more humane alternative—using the court system to resolve disputes. Sadly, that method is increasingly becoming too expensive and cumbersome for people to use.

Some commentators argue that today, people can more readily have the record corrected or improve their reputations by posting good things about themselves online. But it is hard to manipulate Google and other search engines to make the good information crowd out the bad. The problem is that bad information is often more interesting and juicy—and hence more popular. And popularity is the key to getting information to the top of search engine results. Many people have short attention spans and don't care to dig to find out the boring truth or other facts about a person.

The Threat of the Lawsuit

The law works best when it can hover as a threat in the background but allow most problems to be worked out informally. The threat of the lawsuit helps to keep people in check. Without the lawsuit threat, people who defame other people or invade their privacy can just thumb their nose at any complaints.

The problem, of course, is how to have lawsuits serve as a credible threat without being brought inappropriately. Under our current legal system, we have remedies for defamation and invasion of privacy, but . . . these remedies are currently quite limited in their effectiveness, especially the law of privacy. The current law is too limited and restricted to serve as a tenable threat in many situations.

Daniel J. Solove, The Future of Reputation: Gossip, Rumor, and Privacy on the Internet. *New Haven, CT: Yale University Press, 2007, p. 123.*

We need to have an outlet in civilized society for people to vindicate their reputations. We need to have some meaningful way to prevent defamation and invasion of privacy. Otherwise, people will spread all sorts of damaging rumors and gossip about each other online, and victims will return to self-help methods. That would be a big step backwards.

In Kenya, the Media Is Unduly Silenced by Defamation Law

Edwin Mulochi

In the following viewpoint, Edwin Mulochi argues that although it is important to ensure that arbiters of the law are not corrupt in order to deliver justice, it is also important that the laws they must enforce are fair. Mulochi claims that the current law of defamation favors too much privacy for public officials, essentially preventing the media from reporting on important information without risking a lawsuit. He concludes that Kenya needs to live up to its own constitutional commitment to freedom of the press by reforming the law on defamation. Mulochi is legal officer and sub-editor at Radio Africa.

As you read, consider the following questions:

1. According to Mulochi, why is replacing corrupt judges not enough to ensure justice in Kenya?
2. What US Supreme Court case does Mulochi cite in support of his view that defamation law must uphold freedom of the press?
3. According to the author, what article of the Constitution of Kenya guarantees freedom of the press?

Edwin Mulochi, "Defamation Law Needs to Be Reviewed," *Star* (Kenya), May 25, 2012. Copyright © 2012 by the Star Publications Ltd. All rights reserved. Republished with permission.

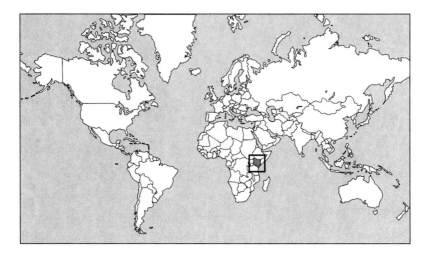

Right from the inception of time, the need for clearly defined laws to govern man's existence and his relationship with all around him has never been in dispute.

The Impact of the Law

We all agree that fidelity to the law is the surest pathway to an orderly and harmonious society. It is to the law that the society turns to, even the scales of justice, whenever they are disturbed.

But when the law itself turns out to be oppressive, one cannot help but shudder at the thought of living in a society governed by it. Life becomes short and brutish. Matters are not made any better by arbiters whose commitment to upholding the rule of law is seriously in question. In an attempt to stave off such a scenario in Kenya, vetting of judges and magistrates is currently in progress. This exercise was long overdue granted the turpitude and sheer averseness to justice that had become the defining hallmarks of the Kenyan judiciary.

Be that as it may, it is my humble submission that ridding the judiciary of judges of questionable character and replacing them with men and women whose fidelity to the law is not in doubt will not guarantee us a society in which justice is reigning supreme. Doing so is not an end but a means to an end. Those conversant with Kenyan laws are unanimous that most of them are not only annoyingly old-fashioned but oppressive as well. Some predate the colonial and even pre-colonial periods. Precedent established out of such laws only serves to perpetuate oppression. Judicial officers, especially in the lower courts, have no option but to apply the precedent established by the higher court.

The Law of Defamation

Take the law of defamation, for instance. A comparison of our law of defamation and that of advanced democracies like the US, Britain among others, leaves one aghast at our unwillingness to make right what is manifestly wrong. Bearing in mind the extremely critical role played by the media, the US carried out the First Amendment of its Constitution.

The motivation behind this amendment was to uphold the freedom of the press. In 1964 in *New York Times Co. v. Sullivan*, the US Supreme Court held that public officials could only win a suit for libel after demonstrating "actual malice" on the part of reporters or publishers. Actual malice was defined as "knowledge that the information was false" or that it was published with "reckless disregard of whether it was false or not". Currently this decision also applies to individuals who are not necessarily public officials but wield considerable clout. The standard for private individuals remains considerably lower.

In 1988 in *Hustler Magazine v. Falwell*, the US Supreme Court further ruled that satire, however scathing and ruffling, is protected by the First Amendment and cannot sustain a defamation suit. It overruled a decision by the jury to award [Jerry] Falwell, a well-known American preacher, $200,000 in damages.

Consequently in the US, there is no demarcation between a public figure's public and private life. The public has a right to thoroughly scrutinise the private and public life of their leaders. And who can fault them anyway? Is it not the right of the public to know who they are entrusting the reins of leadership with? How can they know who they are about to elect or appoint to high office unless he or she comes under the public microscope? And why would anyone who is motivated by a desire to offer sound leadership frown at the prospect of his would-be subjects knowing who he or she is? A public figure can hardly succeed in a defamation suit in the US. This is the law in the world's superpower and I dare say that is how it should be across the globe.

A comparison of our law of defamation and that of advanced democracies ... leaves one aghast at our unwillingness to make right what is manifestly wrong.

Back home we are still steeped in the erroneous mentality that a leader's private life is a no-go zone for the media. As a result, whenever influential individuals sue the media for defamation, they are almost guaranteed of a substantial amount of money in damages. The Kenyan High Court has established a precedent whereby at the very outset of a libel suit, the media is presumed to be on the wrong. There is this misplaced perception that anyone that has been painted in a negative light by the media has suffered irreparable harm and is entitled to damages.

A Dangerous Trend

But the question we should ponder, as a country is, between public interest and private interest, which one should take precedence? Is it not logical that people fronting themselves for leadership positions be exposed for who they truly are? And who is better placed to serve as a window through which

Kenyans can have a glimpse into their leaders' private lives other than the media? True, the media may once in a while go overboard. But should it not be excused given the centrality of the role it plays?

It is time courts guard against being used by prominent people to gag the media.

Lest it escapes our attention, article 34 [of the Constitution of Kenya] guarantees freedom of the press. It cushions the media from unnecessary interference or censure by the state. Article 24, the limitation clause, further states that this right shall not be limited except in accordance with the law and then only to the extent that the limitation is reasonable and justifiable in an open and democratic society based on human dignity, equality and freedom, taking into account all relevant factors.

Despite these clear provisions of the country's fundamental law, the obsession with censuring the media is still at a record high. The jurisprudence from our courts leaves one chagrined at the humongous fines slapped on media houses whenever they are sued for defamation. This has encouraged public figures to scurry to the courts whenever their underhand dealings are exposed by the media.

Needless to say, this [is] an unfortunate and dangerous trend. It makes nonsense of Kenyans' right to information as enshrined in article 35 of the Constitution. It is time courts guard against being used by prominent people to gag the media. The defamation act is also in urgent need of reform to accord with the Constitution.

In Canada, Protection of Privacy Is Compromising Public Access to Information

Laura Kane and Diana Zlomislic

In the following viewpoint, the authors report on issues raised by Irwin Elman, Ontario's Advocate for Children and Youth. Elman complains that the provincial act intended to protect the privacy and legal rights of the child prevents him from identifying any child under provincial protection without the consent of the child, even though some children have died and require inquiries into their death. Elman suggests that not being able to attach a name to an inquest jury recommendation allows the agency handling the case of the child to ignore the recommendation intended to improve conditions. A lawyer involved in an inquest case agrees that although privacy is important, it is more important to have inquest recommendations implemented. Laura Kane and Diana Zlomislic are staff reporters for the Toronto Star, *Canada's highest circulation newspaper.*

As you read, consider the following questions:

1. According to the authors, where have the deaths of the children occurred?

Laura Kane and Diana Zlomislic, "Many Recommendations from Child Death Inquests Never Carried Out," *The Toronto Star*, January 9, 2013. Copyright © 2013 by the Toronto Star. All rights reserved. Republished with permission.

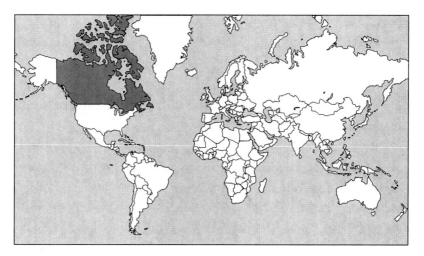

2. According to the authors, what will happen during the Ashley Smith inquest?

3. According to the authors, how many recommendations have been made since 1995? What percentage has been implemented?

Hundreds of key recommendations to prevent the deaths of children in custody have been ignored or rejected by government agencies, the *Toronto Star* has learned.

Agencies responsible for protecting young wards are shielded from public scrutiny once an inquest ends through "bizarre" privacy legislation that forces the office of Ontario's children's advocate to keep secret any information that might identify a youth.

"It's bizarre," said Irwin Elman, Ontario's Advocate for Children and Youth. "While the inquest has been public and the record is public, I cannot identify the person publicly and must even go so far as to not identify agencies."

On Thursday, his office will launch a new online database—the only one of its kind in Canada—that tracks inquest recommendations into the deaths of children in custody. Many of these deaths have occurred in jails or within the child welfare system. In the past 18 years, there have been 26 such cases.

But the provincial act that created Elman's position means that a great deal of relevant information will be missing from this new public record.

The act forbids him from identifying any child under provincial protection without his or her consent. And because it is impossible to obtain consent from a dead child, his office has been forced to redact from the database any information that could potentially identify anyone under the age of 18.

This includes exact dates, locations and the names of provincial ministries, associations, government-funded programs and service providers involved in a child's death.

... because it is impossible to obtain consent from a dead child, [Elman's] office has been forced to redact from the database any information that could potentially identify anyone under the age of 18.

Elman said he has repeatedly asked the Ministry of Children and Youth Services to change the act but it has refused. "I can't imagine (the act) was written this way on purpose," he said.

Paradoxically, the Ashley Smith inquest will attract frenzied media coverage when it begins on Monday but he will be barred from revealing her identity.

"This person who has had their name and photo splashed across televisions and newspapers, to say we're not going to allow him to identify her, it's ludicrous," he said.

Ministry spokesperson Gloria Bacci-Puhl said the confidentiality provisions of the act were crafted in consultation with the Information and Privacy Commissioner to protect the privacy and legal rights of the child.

After an inquest, any agency subject to a recommendation is given a year by the coroner to act. Of the 1,635 recommendations made since 1995, only 17 per cent had been implemented. Another 24 per cent were listed as "had or will be implemented."

About 26 per cent of agencies did not make their response available to the coroner. Another 5 per cent had no response or a response that could not be evaluated.

Keeping tabs on recommendations through an online database will, Elman believes, force government agencies to be more accountable.

"This database is us saying that as a province we owe it to the children who have died. This is their legacy," he said. "I hope it pushes all the sectors towards taking these recommendations seriously."

Many of the recommendations cited in Elman's database have been repeated over and over by inquest juries.

Recommendations are not drawn from "thin air," says Michael Blain, counsel for Ontario's chief coroner. Juries "must have heard some evidence to support the recommendation."

Since 1995, at least seven different inquests have pressed for greater access to mental health assessments, treatment services and appropriate placements for youth with mental health issues.

Three-year-old Matthew Reid was in the care of a foster home affiliated with the Children's Aid Society in St. Catharines, Ont. when a 14-year-old girl, a new ward at the home, fatally smothered him.

The inquest concluded in late 2010. So far, none of the jury's 45 recommendations have been implemented.

A key recommendation arising from that hearing focused on improved information-sharing between government agencies.

Elman is skeptical of agencies that claim to be in the process of adopting jury recommendations.

"I would argue that if they're still thinking about it 15 years later, that means it's not going to be implemented," he said.

One unnamed child welfare agency pledged to hire a quality assurance manager after the death of one of its wards. The job has yet to be filled due to "front line workload demands and budgetary restraints." That recommendation was made more than 10 years ago.

David Meffe, 16, hanged himself while on "suicide watch" at Toronto Youth Assessment Centre in 2002. The inquest into his death revealed that jail staff had virtually no medical history for the youth; it recommended that medical records be attached to court-ordered assessments.

"While I think privacy is important, the more important work is to have inquest juries make recommendations and have them be listened to. . . ."

But this did not happen for Pickering's Gleb Alfyorov, 17, who hanged himself with his shoelaces in an Ontario jail in 2008 while awaiting a psychiatric assessment. In fact, eight other juries had already made the same pleas for change that they made in Alfyorov's inquest in 2011.

Michael Fraleigh, lawyer for David Meffe's family, said privacy must be balanced against the greater good.

"While I think privacy is important, the more important work is to have inquest juries make recommendations and have them be listened to," he said.

"If there is a name and even a face associated with the person who has passed away . . . it brings it home."

Periodical and Internet Sources Bibliography

The following articles have been selected to supplement the diverse views presented in this chapter.

Jonathan Burchell	"The Legal Protection of Privacy in South Africa: A Transplantable Hybrid," *Electronic Journal of Comparative Law*, March 2009.
Siobhain Butterworth	"Privacy, Libel or Protection of Reputation?," *Butterworth and Bowcott on Law Blog—Guardian*, April 8, 2011. www.theguardian.com.
Saikat Datta	"The Walls Have Ears," *Outlook* (India), July 11, 2011.
George Eaton	"Clegg Impresses on Libel Reform," *New Statesman*, January 7, 2011.
Peter Foster	"China's Bugged Taxis and the Right to Privacy," *Telegraph* (UK), September 22, 2010.
Chip Le Grand	"Libel Laws 'Must Apply' to New Media," *Australian*, December 23, 2010.
Paul McKenzie, Jingxiao Fang, and Arthur Dicker	"China: Seeking Balance in Regulating Data Privacy," *Forbes*, April 20, 2011.
Aggery Mutambo	"Media Fights 'Excessive' Libel Awards," *Daily Nation* (Kenya), February 17, 2012.
Michael Pearce	"Legislate the Right to Privacy," *Sydney Morning Herald* (Australia), July 27, 2011.
Geoffrey Wheatcroft	"Privacy, Libel and the Case of Dominique Strauss-Kahn," *National Interest*, May 19, 2011.
Kenny Wong and Eugene Low	"Legal Protection of Privacy Is Scattered Among Various Laws," *South China Morning Post* (Hong Kong), November 21, 2012.

For Further Discussion

Chapter 1

1. Lymari Morales claims that the majority of Americans are willing to sacrifice some privacy during air travel for the sake of security. How do you think Daniel J. Solove would respond to this data? Does public opinion matter in this debate? Explain your reasoning.

2. All of the authors of the viewpoints in this chapter discuss government surveillance or policies that impinge on privacy. In thinking about how much privacy can be sacrificed for security, is the trustworthiness of a particular government relevant? Use support from at least one of the viewpoints to defend your view.

Chapter 2

1. Drawing on the viewpoints in this chapter, identify at least two differences between the privacy protections related to technology in the United States compared to that of Europe.

Chapter 3

1. Kate Smurthwaite claims women's privacy rights will be violated if the United Kingdom's Department of Health releases statistics on late-term abortions. Do you think such statistics should be released? Explain your reasoning.

2. Pew Research Center and Damian Ugwu explore how the right to privacy may protect same-sex marriage. Raise one objection to the claim that a right to privacy supports the right to same-sex marriage.

Chapter 4

1. Authors in this chapter take varying positions on how to balance the right to privacy with the public's right to know. Give an example of a recent news story where privacy and the public right to know had to be balanced. Drawing upon at least two of the authors in this chapter, explain why you think the right to privacy or the public's right to know is stronger.

Organizations to Contact

The editors have compiled the following list of organizations concerned with the issues debated in this book. The descriptions are derived from materials provided by the organizations. All have publications or information available for interested readers. The list was compiled on the date of publication of the present volume; the information provided here may change. Be aware that many organizations take several weeks or longer to respond to inquiries, so allow as much time as possible.

African Commission on Human and Peoples' Rights

31 Bijilo Annex Layout, Kombo North District
Western Region, Banjul   PO Box 673
   Gambia
(220) 4410 505 • fax: (220) 4410 504
e-mail: au-banjul@africa-union.org
website: www.achpr.org

The African Commission on Human and Peoples' Rights interprets the African Charter on Human and Peoples' Rights, aiming to promote and protect the rights of Africans. The African Commission on Human and Peoples' Rights undertakes studies and research on African human rights; organizes seminars, symposia, and conferences; disseminates information; and makes recommendations to African governments. Available at its website is the text of the African Charter on Human and Peoples' Rights, which includes the protection of several civil liberties.

American Civil Liberties Union (ACLU)

125 Broad Street, 18th Floor, New York, NY   10004
(212) 549-2500
e-mail: infoaclu@aclu.org
website: www.aclu.org

The American Civil Liberties Union (ACLU) is a national organization that works to defend Americans' civil rights as guaranteed in the US Constitution. The ACLU works in courts, legislatures, and communities to defend First Amendment rights, the right to equal protection, the right to due process, and the right to privacy. The ACLU publishes the semiannual newsletter *Civil Liberties Alert* as well as numerous briefings and reports, including "Surveillance Under the Patriot Act."

Amnesty International
1 Easton Street, London   WC1X 0DW
  United Kingdom
(44) 20 7413 5500 • fax: (44) 20 7956 1157
website: www.amnesty.org

Amnesty International is a worldwide movement of people who campaign for internationally recognized human rights for all. Amnesty International conducts research and generates action to prevent and end grave abuses of human rights and to demand justice for those whose rights have been violated. At its website, Amnesty International has numerous publications on a variety of human rights issues, including "Nigeria: 'Same Gender' Marriage Ban Would Attack Rights: Bill Would Invade Privacy, Threaten Broad Range of Activists."

Big Brother Watch
55 Tufton Street, London   SW1P 3QL
  United Kingdom
44 (0) 207 340 6030
e-mail: info@bigbrotherwatch.org.uk
website: www.bigbrotherwatch.org.uk

Big Brother Watch is an organization that aims to challenge policies that threaten privacy, freedoms, and civil liberties, and to expose the scale of the surveillance state in the United Kingdom. Big Brother Watch produces research regarding the erosion of civil liberties, the expansion of surveillance powers, the growth of the database state, and the misuse of personal information.

Electronic Frontier Foundation (EFF)
815 Eddy Street, San Francisco, CA   94109
(415) 436-9333 • fax: (415) 436-9993

e-mail: info@eff.org
website: www.eff.org

The Electronic Frontier Foundation (EFF) works to promote the public interest in critical battles affecting digital rights. EFF provides legal assistance in cases where it believes it can help shape the law. EFF publishes a newsletter and reports such as "Defending Privacy at the U.S. Border: A Guide for Travelers Carrying Digital Devices."

Electronic Privacy Information Center (EPIC)

1718 Connecticut Avenue NW, Suite 200
Washington, DC   20009
(202) 483-1140 • fax: (202) 483-1248
website: www.epic.org

The Electronic Privacy Information Center (EPIC) is a public interest research center aimed at protecting privacy, the First Amendment, and constitutional values. EPIC engages in research aimed at focusing public attention on emerging civil liberties issues. EPIC publishes an online newsletter on civil liberties in the information age, the *EPIC Alert*.

Human Rights Watch (HRW)

350 Fifth Avenue, 34th Floor, New York, NY   10118-3299
(212) 290-4700 • fax: (212) 736-1300
website: www.hrw.org

Human Rights Watch (HRW) is dedicated to protecting the human rights of people around the world. HRW investigates human rights abuses, educates the public, and works to change policy and practice. Among its numerous publications is the report "Rights Out of Reach."

Liberty

26–30 Strutton Ground, London   SW1P 2HR
   United Kingdom
(44) 20 7403 3888
website: www.liberty-human-rights.org.uk

Liberty, also known as the National Council for Civil Liberties, is a nonparty membership organization aiming to protect fundamental rights and freedoms in the United Kingdom. Liberty campaigns to protect basic rights and freedoms through the courts, in Parliament, and in the wider community. Available at its website, Liberty publishes campaign materials, speeches, policy papers, fact sheets, and articles, including "The Case Against ID Cards."

Privacy International
46 Bedford Row, London   WC1R 4LR
  United Kingdom
(44) 20 7242 2836
e-mail: info@privacy.org
website: www.privacyinternational.org

Privacy International's mission is to defend the right to privacy around the world as well as to fight surveillance and other intrusions into private life by governments and corporations. Privacy International works at national and international levels to ensure strong legal protections for privacy and seeks ways to protect privacy through the use of technology. Privacy International conducts research to raise awareness about threats to privacy and publishes reports on surveillance methods and tactics, such as "A New Dawn: Privacy in Asia."

Privacy Rights Clearinghouse
PO Box 2126, San Diego, CA   92103
(619) 298-3396
website: www.privacyrights.org

Privacy Rights Clearinghouse is a nonprofit organization aimed at providing consumer information and consumer advocacy on issues of privacy. Privacy Rights Clearinghouse responds to privacy-related complaints from consumers and advocates for consumers' privacy rights in local, state, and federal public policy proceedings. Privacy Rights Clearinghouse publishes numerous fact sheets on consumer privacy issues, available at its website.

United Nations (UN)
One United Nations Plaza, New York, NY   10017
(212) 906-5000 • fax: (212) 906-5001
website: www.un.org

The United Nations (UN) is an international organization of 193 member states committed to maintaining international peace and security; developing friendly relations among nations; and promoting social progress, better living standards, and human rights. The UN works around the world in peacekeeping, peace building, conflict prevention, and humanitarian assistance. The UN publishes numerous annual human development reports and other publications, available at its website.

Bibliography of Books

William P. Bloss — *Under a Watchful Eye: Privacy Rights and Criminal Justice*. Santa Barbara, CA: Praeger, 2009.

John C. Domino — *Civil Rights and Liberties in the 21st Century*. New York: Longman, 2010.

Martin R. Dowding — *Privacy: Defending an Illusion*. Lanham, MD: Scarecrow Press, 2011.

A.C. Grayling — *Liberty in the Age of Terror: A Defence of Civil Liberties and Enlightenment Values*. New York: Bloomsbury, 2011.

David L. Hudson Jr. — *The Right to Privacy*. New York: Chelsea House, 2009.

R. Kakungulu-Mayambala — *Privacy, Data Protection, and National Security: Analyzing the Right to Privacy in Correspondence and Communication in Uganda*. Kampala: Human Rights and Peace Centre, Faculty of Law, Makerere University, 2009.

Garret Keizer — *Privacy*. New York: Picador, 2012.

Saul Levmore and Martha C. Nussbaum, eds. — *The Offensive Internet: Speech, Privacy, and Reputation*. Cambridge, MA: Harvard University Press, 2010.

Rebecca MacKinnon — *Consent of the Networked: The Worldwide Struggle for Internet Freedom*. New York: Basic Books, 2012.

Jon L. Mills — *Privacy: The Lost Right*. New York: Oxford University Press, 2008.

Evgeny Morozov   *The Net Delusion: The Dark Side of Internet Freedom.* New York: Public Affairs, 2011.

Cath Senker   *Privacy and Surveillance.* New York: Rosen Central, 2012.

Daniel J. Solove   *The Future of Reputation: Gossip, Rumor, and Privacy on the Internet.* New Haven, CT: Yale University Press, 2007.

Daniel J. Solove   *Nothing to Hide: The False Tradeoff Between Privacy and Security.* New Haven, CT: Yale University Press, 2011.

Adriana de Souza e Silva and Jordan Frith   *Mobile Interfaces in Public Spaces: Locational Privacy, Control, and Urban Sociability.* New York: Routledge, 2012.

Robin Tudge   *The No-Nonsense Guide to Global Surveillance.* Toronto: Between the Lines, 2011.

Paul Tweed   *Privacy and Libel Law: The Clash with Press Freedom.* Haywards Heath, England: Bloomsbury Professional, 2012.

Raymond Wacks   *Privacy: A Very Short Introduction.* New York: Oxford University Press, 2010.

Hao Wang — *Protecting Privacy in China: A Research on China's Privacy Standards and the Possibility of Establishing the Right to Privacy and the Information Privacy Protection Legislation in Modern China.* New York: Springer, 2011.

Samantha R. Weber, ed. — *Promoting Global Internet Freedom.* Hauppauge, NY: Nova Science Publishers, 2010.

Elia Zureik et al. — *Surveillance, Privacy, and the Globalization of Personal Information: International Comparisons.* Montreal, Quebec: McGill-Queen's University Press, 2010.

Index

Geographic headings and page numbers in **boldface** refer to viewpoints about that country or region.

CPSIA information can be obtained
at www.ICGtesting.com
Printed in the USA
FFOW01n0453070214
3478FF

9 780737 769135